Anna Fuller

Pratt Portraits

Sketched in a New England Suburb

Anna Fuller

Pratt Portraits
Sketched in a New England Suburb

ISBN/EAN: 9783744677745

Printed in Europe, USA, Canada, Australia, Japan

Cover: Foto ©Thomas Meinert / pixelio.de

More available books at **www.hansebooks.com**

PRATT PORTRAITS

PORTRAITS

SKETCHED IN A NEW ENGLAND
SUBURB ❧ BY ANNA FULLER

Illustrated by George Sloane

G. P. PUTNAM'S SONS
NEW YORK AND LONDON
THE KNICKERBOCKER PRESS
1899

The Knickerbocker Press, New York

CONTENTS.

NOTE.

It is owing to the courtesy of Messrs. Harper and Brothers that I am permitted to include in this volume seven sketches which have previously appeared in *Harper's Bazar;* namely, "Aunt Betsy's Photographs," "Harriet," "Ben's Wife," "The Schoolmarm," "Old Lady Pratt," "Well Matched," and "Uncle Bobby."

A. F.

ILLUSTRATIONS.

PRATT PORTRAITS.

AUNT BETSY'S PHOTOGRAPHS.

AUNT BETSY lived with her mother, Old Lady Pratt, in a small house in Green Street. Small as the house was, she had never got over the impression that it was rather large, and very handsome. Forty-five years ago, before she lost her hearing, Aunt Betsy, then little Betty Pratt, had heard her mother pronounce it to be "in every respect superior" to the house they had left, though that had been "a very desirable residence in its day." It stood on a quiet little side street, where there were no pretentious neighbors to put it out of countenance; a street which slumbered on, so undisturbed by the bustle of the town a few blocks away that Aunt Betsy used sometimes to wonder whether it were not "a little hard o' hearin' too."

The "new house," as she still called it in her own thoughts, was long and rambling, presenting a narrow end to the street, upon which only the staircase windows looked, and then elongating itself surprisingly, away back into what would have been the backyard had not the wood-shed crowded itself up to the very fence. This obliged them to stretch their clothes-line across the long, narrow grass-plot, which followed the line of the house from back to front—a thing which was something of a trial to Aunt Betsy. She never thought it quite modest to hang out your under-garments in full view of the passers-by, and she had sometimes wished that a hedge might be planted across the space, just beyond the green side-door. But being very much in awe of her mother, she had never ventured to suggest any such innovation, and had contented herself with a persistent effort to have the sheets and table-cloths hung on the front line. As she did not assign any reason for this arrangement, it is no wonder that Eliza, Mrs. Pratt's " girl "—a maiden of some sixty odd summers,—regarded it as a "whim of Miss Betsy's," and was not always mindful of so arbitrary a rule.

Aunt Betsy lived in a very small world indeed, and her small world was entirely overshadowed by the strong and rather severe influence of her mother. She was but ten years old when the narrow barriers of her life were fixed irrevocably about her soul.

Only a few days after they moved into the new house the little daughter, the youngest of six children, slipped on the steep, narrow backstairs, and fell from top to bottom. From that time she became almost totally deaf. Whether at the same time her faculties were deadened, or whether they had become dull from want of incentive from without, no one knows. Certain it is that she was never the lively, intelligent child that Mrs. Pratt had every right to expect a child of hers to be.

She was now a tall, rather corpulent woman, with somewhat flabby cheeks, and little appearance of "backbone," wherein she presented a striking contrast to her small, upright mother, who even in her eighty-fifth year never leaned back in her chair, and whose bright black eyes could startle Betsy, with a look which seemed positively shrill to the poor old woman, in the eternal silence of her consciousness.

For she grew to be an old woman after a time. She saw her brothers and sisters leave their home, one after another, and make new homes for themselves ; her father, who had been gentle with her, "departed hence," and, last of all, Ben, her favorite brother, took to himself a wife, and moved into Bliss Street.

Ben was a kindly soul, of few words, who had always got on better than any one else with Betsy. For instead of trying to talk to her, and getting impatient when she did not hear, he had a way of turning upon her now and then a broad, beaming smile as delightful as a whole conversation. On his wedding day he made Betsy a present, which remained her dearest possession as long as she lived. It was a large glass pin, containing a lock of her father's hair, and bordered with a row of small seed-pearls. On the golden back was inscribed, in old English letters,

𝔅. 𝔓. from 𝔅. 𝔓.
A Parting Gift.

She wore it on Sundays, and when the minister came to tea, and at the christenings and weddings of her nieces and nephews. The rest of the time it reposed in a small satin-lined box, together with a carnelian ring which her mother thought she was too old to wear, and a stray onyx sleeve-button which had belonged to her father.

She felt sorry to have Ben go, and she told him so, in an unsteady voice that went to the kind fellow's heart; but then she supposed it was "natural enough," and she submitted, quite uncomplainingly, to the life alone with her sharp-eyed mother, which was to reach on and on into the future.

Happily, Betsy did not think much about the future. She was a placid soul, not realizing very clearly how much brighter other lives were than hers. She loved her canary-bird and the great "Malty" cat, Topsy by name, which attained to a fabulous age, living in undisputed possession of the one really comfortable chair in the sitting-

room.   And, above all, she found companionship
in her flowers.   Every one gave her slips and seed-
lings, and marvelled at her success in raising
them.   The sunny south window in the wood-
shed was the nursery for these pets of hers, and
not until they were fairly flowering were they
promoted to the green wire stand in the sitting-
room.   The neighbors used to praise her skill
and ask her advice, and even her mother would
sometimes betray a pride in this " faculty " of
Betsy's.

" Betsy," she would say, when Mrs. Baxter
had come in with her knitting to pass the afternoon—" Betsy, you go out into the wood-shed
and fetch in that little flower that blowed this
mornin'.   Mis' Baxter would like to see it,
mebbe."

She did not succeed so well with the children
growing up about her.   She was a little shy of
them, of their gay chatter, which she could not
understand, and their childish egotism.   They all
loved Grandma, or, as she had now become,
Great-grandmamma Pratt.   She made such good
jokes, and laughed, and was interested in all
their doings.   But Aunt Betsy just sat there with
her worsted-work, and did n't hear when she
was spoken to unless you quite shouted in her
ear, and then she jumped in such a funny way,
and seemed so flustered.   Why, she could n't even
" make a cheese " for them, when the big hoops
came into fashion, by twirling round and round

and then suddenly sitting plump down on the floor with her skirts rising in billows about her. Aunt Emmeline could do it, and Aunt Martha, and 'most any body, but Aunt Betsy said it made her head giddy. Aunt Betsy was "no good."

Sometimes, when Betsy found how startling and troublesome these small specimens of humanity were, she was almost reconciled to being an old maid. She knew that her mother was a good deal mortified at having a child who had never "had an offer," and she felt hot and uncomfortable as often as she thought of a certain temptation which had assailed her many years ago. It was when the neighborhood was stirred and shocked by the sudden death of young Alfred Williams, an amiable though impecunious member of Green Street society, who had been left over, as it were, from among her sister Jane's admirers. Betsy was at that time about twenty-one years old, and Alfred had continued coming in pretty regularly to tea of an evening after the disappearance of Jane from the family circle. The goodness of the fare may have been an attraction, or perhaps he really liked Betsy, though he gave no sign. However that may have been, his visits had not passed unnoted by the neighbors, and the morning he died Mrs. Baxter came in to discuss the news.

"He was a very well favored young man, I am sure," said she, "and a great loss to our circle. Dr. Baxter says he has heard that his employers had entire confidence in him. And, by-the-way," she added, turning to Betsy, and raising her voice to its highest pitch, "I always thought that Alfred had rather a leaning to you, Betsy."

This speech threw Betsy into such an unwonted tremor and flutter that she blushed violently, and looked guilty of a hundred tender passages.

The moment their visitor had departed, Mrs. Pratt beckoned her daughter to her side on the sofa and asked, in her penetrating voice, "Did he ever *say* anything, Betsy?"

I fancy that Betsy, at the moment, would have given half her life's purchase to say "Yes"; but something within her which no limitations could stunt, a perfectly well developed New England conscience, compelled her to answer :

"No, Mother, he never said a word."

So the stigma of the unsought rested upon poor Betsy, and her last chance was lost of rising in her mother's esteem.

Before she was forty her mother put her into caps, which she never changed the fashion of. They were flat on top and very bunchy at the sides, with purple or green ribbons, which bobbed up and down when she moved her head. She got a habit of letting her head "joggle" a little as she bent over her worsted-work or tatting, much to the disgust of her mother, who tried to break her of it. But her mother's admonitions used to frighten her so that she lost control of herself in that peremptory little woman's presence, and her head only shook the harder. When she was alone in her room she could almost always get it steady again. She used to sit in front of the glass, seeing how still she could hold her head; and, curiously enough, this study of her own countenance, so new and yet so fascinating, developed a singular vanity in her which no one would have dreamed of suspecting. Especially of a Sunday, when she had on her "shot-silk" gown, with Brother Ben's pin fastening the broad flat collar, and when her best cap rested on her gray locks, she would look deprecatingly at her fat, amiable old face, and wonder if blue eyes were not "'most as pretty as black," and whether, if she had not been so deaf, she too might not have had offers like the other women she knew.

It was about this time—that is, when Aunt Betsy was well on in the fifties—that photography was first invented, and her brothers and sisters began coming in with little card pictures of themselves and their families. All the neighborhood was excited about these wonderful likenesses, to be got at three dollars a dozen, and so much more satisfactory than the old daguerreotypes, which one had to turn this way and that to see them at all. Even Grandma was at last persuaded to sit for hers, and it had been in such demand that two dozen had been ordered on the spot, and they had "gone off like hot cakes," as Brother Ben kept saying over and over again.

Aunt . ;y was never tired of studying these
black-and-white representations of her relatives,
and she secretly cherished a hope that some one
would propose her sitting for hers.   Nobody
thought of such a thing, however, though one of
her sisters gave her a small photograph album
bound in purple cloth.   This did not fill up very
fast, as Grandma always had to have the new photographs, and not many people were prepared to
squander two specimens on one family.   She had
her mother, looking unnaturally meek without
her spectacles, and Brother Ben and Sister Harriet,
besides the youngest babies in the family, whose
mothers really could not refuse the lovely things
to any one who asked for them.   But this was
all.

By and by the new sensation was a little past,
and other subjects of interest came up, lacking
pictorial illustration—subjects in which Aunt
Betsy could not take so intelligent a part.

Now Aunt Betsy had always a little store of
money, which her well-to-do brothers and sisters
kept her supplied with.   Her sister Harriet
particularly was " quite a rich woman," as Old
Lady Pratt took some pride in stating, and rode
in her carriage ; and not infrequently she made
her sister Betsy a present of a quarter or even
half a dollar.   Betsy, who was a hospitable
soul, used to wait upon their guests to the door,
and say, in a tone of mild entreaty, no matter
what the length of the visit might have been :

" Do come agin, when you can stay longer."

In response to which little formula Sister Harriet would often slip a bit of paper currency into her hand, and say ;

" Thank you, Betsy. There ! There 's a trifle for your worsted-work."

And to that purpose the money was usually devoted ; for, so small was Aunt Betsy's world, that even objects of charity seldom found their way into it, and the contribution box, with its mute appeal, never crossed her vision. Her mother had long ago decreed that " there was no sense in Betsy's goin' to meetin'. She could n't hear a syllable, and it was a shame to go to the Lord's House jest to stare about you."

So the money which might have swelled the missionary exchequer went to the purchase of very brilliant colored worsteds, which were always utilized in the following manner : Aunt Betsy would work on canvas, in black cross-stitch, the outline of hearts, ingeniously arranged, so that the lobe of one furnished the point for the next above it. These hearts were filled in, each with a different colored worsted, the small diamond-shaped spaces between being wrought in bright yellow silk, and thus pin-cushions and sofa pillows were made and sown broadcast throughout the family.

Betsy was also skilled in making tape trimming for underclothes, and she had a wooden frame on which she sometimes embroidered rather unsubstantial lace. But she much preferred to work in colors. " Colors are so speaking," as she used to say to herself. Her special pride was a sofa cushion she once worked for Sister Harriet, which contained three hundred and twenty-four hearts, no two of which were done in the same shade of worsted.

There came a time when Aunt Betsy felt that if she did not have her picture taken before she grew any older and shakier, it would be too great a disappointment ; and one day, when her mother was gone to "pass the afternoon with Harriet," Aunt Betsy, feeling as though she were committing a theft, took three dollars from her upper bureau drawer, tied up the bandbox containing her best cap, and, arrayed in her "shot silk " gown and Brother Ben's pin, set out with palpitating heart for the photograph saloon. It was her first visit to the place, but she knew the entrance well.

The short walk was accomplished all too soon, and long before she had gathered courage she found herself confronted with the great glass case, filled with specimens of the photographer's art, on which she had often gazed with admiration. As she stopped a moment to study the stony or smirking features of her fellow-townsmen, she received an unexpected shock. In the very middle of the case, a strangely familiar countenance met her eye, and seemingly returned her gaze with the light of recognition. The photograph was enlarged to about ten times its normal size, and had thus become a startlingly realistic presentment of the original. It was no other than Sister Harriet, with her jet-black "false front," her white muslin "bosom," and the large diamond ring on the forefinger of her right hand. Betsy's heart almost stopped beating as she gazed, fascinated, into the familiar face; but its expression of fixed self-complacency could not, even to her guilty conscience, seem disapproving, and somewhat encouraged she respectfully took her leave of it, and began the ascent of the four flights of stairs which led to the photographic Parnassus.

Arrived, panting and perturbed, at the door, which opened directly at the head of the stairs, it was some time before she could make up her mind to go into the mysterious sanctuary where occult arts were practised; and besides, she kept telling herself that if she were to meet one of her acquaintances she should "sink through the floor." In this respect Fate was kind; for when at last she summoned courage to open the door and go in, she found the room untenanted. A strange uncanny odor greeted her entrance into the bare, empty room, and she looked about her with a vague uneasiness, half expecting to see a wicked magician emerge from the curtained glass door in one corner of the room. To her infinite relief, a meek-looking little man of a blond complexion came forward and politely offered his services.

" Is this Mr. Billings, the photographer ? " she asked, in an awe-struck tone.

" At your service, madam," he replied.   If only Aunt Betsy could have heard the deferential words and tone !

" I came to sit for my photograph."

" Certainly, madam ; certainly.   Will you step into the operating-room ? "

" I am a little hard of hearing," said Aunt Betsy, with an inclination of the head ; and perceiving, after several attempts, that she was indeed " a little hard of hearing," the little man shouted, in a voice that would have done credit to a mastodon : " The *operating-room* is this way."

The ghastly word struck terror to Aunt Betsy's soul, and her head began to shake nervously. " There must be some mistake," she faltered, though speaking with all the dignity she could command.   " I wish to sit for my photograph."

" Certainly, madam ; certainly.   Just step this way, if you please "; and with a reassuring smile and a cheerful alacrity not to be resisted, he led the way into the adjoining room.

It was a dazzlingly bright apartment, with a bare yet cluttered look, which Aunt Betsy could not approve.   There were chairs and tables in meaningless situations, pictured screens leaning helplessly against one another, and the evil-looking tripod mysteriously draped in green baize.

" Mr. Billings, the photographer," disappeared behind the screens, and left Aunt Betsy standing, dazed, in the middle of the room.

Suddenly the mastodon voice at her ear shouted: "Are you fond of foreign travel, ma'am? Here is a very handsome ruin for a background."

Turning, with a start, Aunt Betsy beheld a screen decorated with broken Corinthian columns and a Roman aqueduct. She thought it very fine, but before she had time to confess that she had never been out of Middlevale County, the obliging young man had whisked out a wonderful landscape, representing a majestic water-fall and several impossible trees.

"Perhaps you prefer a bit of nature, ma'am," he roared. That, too, was very beautiful, but both seemed to her a little ambitious for a person who had never seen a water-fall, nor dreamed of a Roman aqueduct. There was a familiar look about those Corinthian pillars, which she associated with Sister Harriet's picture; but then, it would not be presumptuous in Sister Harriet, who might have travelled in foreign parts any time these ten years, if it had not been for that dangerous ocean.

While she was pondering thus on the fitness of things, the indefatigable Mr. Billings produced another screen, covered with grape-vines such as grew on the wood-shed at home. And then, oh, wonder of wonders! he drew forth a wicket gate of the most picturesque description, and placed it alluringly before the grape-vine.

"There, madam!" he shouted, "if you would stand in a natural attitude behind that gate, with your right hand upon the top, as though about to pass through, I think you would find the effect artistic."

This was a long effort for the mastodon voice, but the word "artistic" was distinctly audible, and the young man placed his own hand upon the gate in a manner which appealed so strongly to Aunt Betsy's imagination that she assented timidly to the arrangement. Mr. Billings then kindly anticipated a difficulty which would have seemed to Aunt Betsy insurmountable, by showing her into a small closet, furnished with a looking glass and a gas-jet, where she could remove her bonnet and don her cap without "exposing" herself.

When she returned she found Mr. Billings handling some queer little slates resembling those which the children carried to school. He slipped one into the camera, and then, coming forward, proceeded to station his "subject" in front of the grape-vine, her right hand, in a black lace mitt, reposing upon the wicket gate, and her voluminous skirts spreading on either side. Then a tall iron stand was placed at her back, and a pair of cold prongs inserted under the purple ribbons behind each ear; after which Mr. Billings withdrew behind his camera and enveloped his head in the green baize. For a moment it seemed to Aunt Betsy almost as though he were trifling with her, but when he again emerged, with his face very red and his hair much dishevelled, there was a look of professional gravity and concentration upon his amiable countenance which dispelled such thoughts; and even when he tripped back to her and took her temples delicately between his thumbs and lightly chucked her under the chin to improve the pose, she felt convinced that the sudden flush which mounted to her brow was quite uncalled for.

Having moved off a little, cocked his head first on one side and then on the other, Mr. Billings again retreated beneath the green baize. In a moment he came smiling back, rubbing his hands together and murmuring: "Excellent, really excellent"; and then, in stentorian tones he shouted: "Would you be kind enough to moisten your lips, madam? Thank you. Now fix your eyes on that black spot on the wall. Look pleasant. Yes—very good, very good. Wink freely, but do not move your head."

Oh, the comfort of those iron tongs!

Vaguely wishing that she had such a pair at home, Aunt Betsy braced her untrustworthy head against them and stood in the glaring light, her eyes fixed upon the foolish black spot which danced perplexingly before her, her lips tightly closed, and a strange, unearthly look graven upon her countenance.

When release came, the poor old lady was almost too cramped to move or to feel the exultation natural to a released victim. Truly, the "operating-room" was aptly named, in those first stages of the black-and-white art.

But, a few minutes later, when Aunt Betsy paid her three dollars in advance and engaged to call for the photographs,—"Thank you, I would rather not give my address or have them sent home—I want to surprise my folks,"—a delicious feeling came over her of living in a wonderful age, and of being, at last, fully abreast of the times.

Some days of suppressed excitement passed, and at last the photographs were finished and delivered into her hands, and she knew, with a guilty knowledge, that the time had come for her to "surprise her folks." She hurried home, looking neither to the right nor to the left, the precious package buried in the depths of her pocket, entered the house surreptitiously as a burglar, and crept up to her own room. When the dooı was securely fastened, she took a long breath, and then proceeded, not to examine the pictures, but to put her bonnet and shawl carefully away, smooth her hair with a fine-tooth comb, and adjust her cap before the glass; then she tied on her black silk apron, and sat down by the open window, holding the little package in her hand.

It was a brilliant September day, and she sat looking out into the great horse-chestnut tree before the window. Her father had planted it forty-five years ago, for he liked to have horse-chestnuts "handy." He firmly believed that they would ward off rheumatism if carried in the pocket; and sure enough, as Aunt Betsy reflected, he had never had a twinge of rheumatism in the sixty odd years of his life !

In the horse-chestnut tree was a bird-cote in the shape of a white-steepled " meeting-house." A fat little sparrow, perched on the door-sill of this minute edifice, was chirping sharply. Aunt Betsy watched his agitated little body, but did not hear him chirp. In the yard Eliza, the "girl," was vigorously pumping, causing a stream of water to gush noisily into the pail, and Aunt Betsy could see the neighbor's dog barking vociferously at a cat in a tree. But none of these sounds penetrated the heavy silence in which she was wrapped about. Only the beating of her pulse throbbed in her ears, and in a nervous tremor she delayed opening the package, much as a young girl might delay breaking the seal of a love-letter when once she had it in secure possession. So alike are sensations from totally different causes, and sensations of any kind being rare in Aunt Betsy's experience, she might well linger a little over this one.

But at last she had drawn one of the little cards from the package, and held it in her hand, and as the pleasant south wind fluttered her cap ribbons, and the afternoon sun shone kindly upon her, she looked shyly at her pictured countenance, and a sense of deep satisfaction transfused itself through her.

There was no mistaking the contour of her best cap : and as for the breastpin, she could almost

AUNT BETSY.

count the seed-pearls in the rim, while the "artistic effect" of that wicket-gate seemed to her "too pretty for anything." The rigidity of the attitude quite escaped her uncritical eye, and she failed to observe that the accustomed look of mild benevolence which sat so well on her plain face was here turned to an expression of almost savage intensity, as much out of place as a frown on a rabbit's countenance.

Yes, Aunt Betsy's dream was realized. She held in her hand twelve unmistakable likenesses of her "Sunday things," and they gave her as much pleasure as the most brilliant colored paper-doll had caused her when she was a little girl in the old house, and could hear the delightful rattle of the blue and red and yellow papers. Even a bit of color was not lacking to her new treasures, for the photographer had touched the cheeks of the counterfeit Aunt Betsy with spots of vivid carmine.

A spot almost as bright glowed in each cheek of the flesh-and-blood Aunt Betsy as she descended into the sitting-room, not, indeed, to "surprise her folks." She could not yet rid herself of the feeling of guilt connected with the whole transaction, and she dreaded lest her mother should call her a fool, as she had promptly done whenever her docile daughter had committed any mild indiscretion, such as wishing for a "false front" when her hair became gray, or wondering whether the minister, when he came to tea, might not prefer fancy tarts, such as Sister Harriet's new-fangled cook made, to the old-fashioned mince-pies.

"Betsy, you 're a fool!" when pronounced by Old Lady Pratt, never failed to penetrate the muffled hearing like a gun-shot, and Betsy used to wish within herself that her mother would put it a little differently.

Poor Aunt Betsy had been so promptly put down in her life that she had never before had the sensation of committing an out-and-out indiscretion. Now, at least, she had it, and her mother's quick eye instantly detected the unwonted flush.

"Betsy," cried the alert old lady, "come here. Let me feel your pulse! Goodness me, child! You 're in a high fever! You 've caught a cold! You ain't been settin' by an open window?"

The gray-haired culprit admitted that she had.

"Betsy, you 're a fool! You al'ays was full of romantic notions about open windows. You 'll jest go right straight to bed, and drink a cup of pennyr'yal tea. Do you hear?"

Betsy heard. Old Lady Pratt's reproofs were always audible, even to her, and her commands were not to be questioned. So Aunt Betsy was packed away to bed, while the exultation died out within her, and the old patient compliance returned in its place. She lay there in a gentle apathy, watching the last ray of sunlight die away on the flowered wall, and waiting resignedly for the unsavory dose.

Presently the door opened, and the straight

little figure of Mrs. Pratt entered, well lighted up
by the candle she held in one hand, while in the
other she bore a smoking bowl of tea. Her own
cheeks were somewhat flushed from bending over
the fire. She set the candle on the high bureau,
tasted the tea herself once or twice, and then,
without much ceremony, poured the scalding
draught down her patient's throat; after which
she felt her pulse again, and asked to see her
tongue.

"I declare for 't" she cried, "if you 're not
better a'ready! There never was anything like
my pennyr'yal tea for stoppin' a cold off short!
Now you turn over and go right to sleep, and
you 'll be as good as new in the mornin'."

The old lady meant kindly; but what words
could sound kind, spoken in a high falsetto?
Poor Aunt Betsy! I wonder if she herself realized what she missed in never hearing the voices
of her fellow-creatures in their natural tones. No
one could ever speak tenderly to her, nor sooth-
ingly, nor confidentially. All those softer accents,
so much more eloquent than words, must be forever lost to her; she could only know the voices
of her friends in the harsh, strained pitch which
they must take to reach her ears.

Days and weeks went by after Betsy's wonderful cure and the secret of her escapade was
still her own. She shrank more and more from
confessing what she had done, and yet she was
tortured by the feeling that it had been a "dread-

ful waste of money," if she was going to keep
those twelve photographs for herself. She sometimes thought of confessing the whole thing to
kind Brother Ben, or of boldly offering a "picture" to Sister Harriet ; but, at the very suggestion, her whole family seemed to rise before her
in scorn and derision, and she seemed to hear a
chorus of brothers and sisters, nephews and nieces,
joining in her mother's piercing denunciation,

"You 're a fool, Betsy ! you 're a fool !"

She began to have a distaste for the things, and
to entertain daring thoughts of putting them all
into the kitchen fire. But she knew that would
be an abominably weak and wicked proceeding,
and she was not sufficiently hardened to do it.

It was really wearing upon her. She did not
sleep, as she had been used, from ten o'clock at
night till five or six in the morning ; she lost
her appetite little by little, and her grateful smile
came less readily in response to unintelligible
remarks addressed to her by afternoon callers.
Old Lady Pratt confided to Harriet that she was
"afeard Betsy was goin' to break up early ; she
seemed to be losing her sperit."

Poor Betsy, as though she had ever had any
spirit to lose !

So nearly three months wore away, and Aunt
Betsy began to fear that she had sacrificed her
peace of mind for good and all.

One Sunday afternoon in December, Brother Ben
came in with his youngest daughter Hattie, a girl

about twelve years old. They were both lightly sprinkled with snow, and after tramping about a good deal on the oil-cloth in the entry, they came smiling in, bringing a gust of cold air with them.

"Well, Mother; well Betsy," Ben began, immediately. "Hattie 's got a surprise for you. She 's been having her picture taken again, all dressed up in her Red Riding-hood cape. She looks mighty cute; you just see if she don't."

And Hattie, proud and pleased, exhibited the picture to her admiring elders. The slender, hooded form in the photograph was standing behind the little wicket gate which Aunt Betsy knew so well, and Grandma was much taken with it.

"Well, I never!" she cried. "How cute it is, to be sure! Who but Hattie Pratt would have thought of being taken comin' through a gate?"

And impressed with the weight of her own remark, she repeated it in her shrillest tones to Betsy.

"Who indeed?" thought Betsy, longing, but not daring to lay claim to equal brilliancy.

"It *was* a pretty idea," she said, meekly. "I wish you 'd give me one, Hattie, to put in my photograph album.'

Hattie looked up brightly at her deaf old aunt, and said, with decision, "I don't give these away; I only exchange."

" But, Hattie," said her father, "you 'd give your Aunt Betsy one ! You know she never had her picture taken."

"Then she 'll have to, if she wants mine," said the pert little person.

"What did she say?" asked Aunt Betsy, a great resolution already half formed in her mind.

" She says you 'd better have your own picture taken before you go askin' other people for theirs," said Grandma, not ill-pleased to hear Betsy snubbed for her unreasonableness in wanting a picture all to herself.

It was now or never, and Betsy knew it.

"Very well," she said, rising, and looking an inch taller. "I 'll exchange with you." And she marched out of the room, erect and determined leaving her family speechless with astonishment.

Without giving herself time to think of consequences, she seized her twelve photographs, and hurried back to the sitting-room.

"There !" she said, rather explosively, "you can have your choice, Hattie."

Old Lady Pratt, doubting her senses, seized one of the pictures, looked at it, then looked at Betsy. The likeness was unmistakable ; it was " Betsy all over," as she admitted to herself. But she was so divided in her mind between horror at her daughter's duplicity, and admiration of her "smartness," that she let Ben have the first word. He came nobly to the rescue.

"Well, Betsy!" he cried. "If you ain't a sly one! Think of that, Mother. To go all by herself, as independent as a chipmunk, and have her picture taken! Well, you *have* given us a surprise, Betsy!"

Betsy heard nothing of this, and not daring to look at her mother and Ben, she watched Hattie, who was gazing with the greatest interest at the picture. Presently Hattie looked up into her aunt's troubled face, and with a sudden intuition, perhaps the first movement of genuine sympathy she had ever known, the girl took in the situation. She jumped up, and giving her aunt a hearty kiss, cried:

"Thank you so much, Aunt Betsy. It 's ever so good. I believe I 'd rather have a picture of you than of 'most any body—that I have n't got," she added, truthfully.

Aunt Betsy heard every word of this kind little scream, but she was almost too embarrassed to answer.

"Why, Hattie," she stammered, "I 'm so glad! I did n't know——"

"Oh! you 're a sly one," roared Ben. "I always said you were a sly one, and did n't tell all you knew! Is n't she a sly one, Mother?"

"Well," screamed Mrs. Pratt, "it was mighty clever of you to be taken behind that wicket gate, I must say. And your shot silk has come out beautifully."

Aunt Betsy felt very much as a released convict

must feel if met by a band of music and a delegation of distinguished citizens, announcing to him that he had been elected mayor of the city. From the very start she perceived that those photographs were to be the success of her life. Each member of the family insisted upon having one, and all the neighbors admired them and offered to exchange. Aunt Betsy's album filled up fast. Brother Ben had two dozen more struck off at his own expense, and for days and days Aunt Betsy lived in a delightful flutter of excitement. The most indolent of their visitors would exert herself to scream, "Betsy, I hear you 've been sitting for your picture"; and not a day went by without an exhibition of the ever dwindling number.

The crowning moment came on New Year's Day, when Brother Ben arrived, bringing a mysterious flat parcel, which he presented to his mother, with a roguish side glance at Betsy. She looked on with lively curiosity, but little prepared for what was coming. There, in a shiny black frame, was an enormously enlarged copy of Betsy's picture, in which the pin seemed almost life-size, and the expression of stern determination was fairly appalling.

Perhaps Old Lady Pratt had never felt so fond and proud of Betsy since she was a bright little child like other children, as she did when she gazed upon that "handsome picture."

It was hung up in the best parlor, over the haircloth sofa; and later in the day, when mother and daughter stood side by side before it, the sharp little old lady laid her hand with an affectionate pressure on the other's shoulder, and said: "That 's about the smartest thing you ever did, Betsy, I declare for 't."

And I think Betsy went to bed that night the happiest old woman in Green Street.

II

HARRIET.

HARRIET had always been an authority in her small world ; and it was not such a very small world either, as worlds go.

Not only was she a person of consequence, now, when she was the head of a family and mistress of a fortune—her importance was of longer standing than that. To begin with, she had been the eldest of a family of brothers and sisters, who had looked up to her with an unquestioning respect, which even an eldest sister is by no means sure of inspiring. But Harriet was " her mother's own child," upright and firm, with that natural self-respect which is a law unto itself. Such an advantage, while sparing its possessor many a brush with those in authority, invests him with a nimbus of infallibility very impressive to younger and less well-balanced minds. Mrs. Anson Pratt, to be sure, was not the woman to yield the reins of government to any rival power, yet her daughter Harriet early became her chief adviser in such small matters of family economy and discipline as she thought unworthy the

28

consideration of her husband's larger intelligence.

Under these favoring conditions Harriet grew to be a tall, self-possessed maiden; and as the handsomest and cleverest young woman of his acquaintance, was early wooed and won by the handsome and clever young business man James Spencer.

Indeed prosperity had marked her for its own from her very cradle. For while she was still in undisputed possession of that infant refuge, her mother's bachelor brother, William Kingsbury, had died, leaving to his little niece a legacy of two thousand dollars. This befell in the good old times when two thousand dollars was a tidy sum, and when money, being properly invested, doubled itself faster than is the case to-day. As their family increased in numbers a trifle faster than the family income grew, Anson Pratt and his wife would often remind one another that "Harriet was well provided for." The Pratts were plain, unworldly people, not at all inclined to pay undue deference to riches; yet one is tempted to wonder whether, if the little Harriet's future had been less assured, she might not sometimes have been called Hattie. The fact of never having known the levelling influences of a nickname is in itself not without weight in the sum of one's personal dignity.

During the many prosperous years that had elapsed since she had become Mrs. James Spencer,

Harriet had tasted, one after another, the natural joys and the natural sorrows of life, and now that she was nearing the further boundaries of middle life she had become more and more the practical woman—the woman of affairs ; the woman who was oftener appealed to for counsel than for sympathy. Her smooth "false front," her black eyes, her straight nose and well-closed mouth were all calculated to command respect. She was tall, and she felt her height ; physically as well as mentally and morally she was unbending.

Even her great sorrow, the death of her husband, which had occurred fifteen years previous, had come to be to her a regrettable fact rather than an active emotion. Years and a strong will had done their work.

Yet for many weeks after James Spencer's death Harriet had felt with consternation that she was not self-sufficient. A strange, unreasoning sense of helplessness had oppressed her, which was even harder to bear than her actual grief.

The most vivid memory which she had of her husband's last days was that of a certain gloomy afternoon in November, when she had sat at his bedside, and they had taken counsel together for the last time. It was several days before his death, which they both knew to be close at hand. She had been sitting, erect and self-contained, while her husband slept, sternly denying herself the luxury of grief, simply facing the inevitable with rigid endurance. The rain was pattering

upon the tin roof of the piazza beneath the windows, and the sky was dreary as her thoughts. It
seemed to her afterward that that pattering rain,
which continued persistently for three days, had
worn a groove in her consciousness, causing her
to shrink from the sound as from a physical pain.
Her family wondered that she should have her
piazza roof shingled almost immediately after
James' death, and her mother, Old Lady Pratt,
declared it to be a "downright piece of extravagance," and hoped she "was n't goin' to be disapp'inted in Harriet after all these years." But
Harriet knew that when the shingles dulled the
sound of the pattering drops she could think more
naturally of her trouble, and it was peculiarly
necessary that she should allow nothing to disturb her balance. For the same event which had
taken from her a strong support had also imposed
upon her unaccustomed responsibilities. On that
dreary afternoon, which she remembered so well,
her husband had quietly opened his eyes, and
without making any other movement to indicate
his return to consciousness, he had said : "Harriet, I have left all the money to you."

This simplicity of speech was characteristic of
James Spencer. He had been a genial and rather
demonstrative man in every-day life, but in matters that touched him deeply he disliked effusion.
He could trust his wife to meet him in his own
spirit.

"All, James ?" she queried.

"Yes, all; I leave you to provide for the children according to your judgment."

"It is not the usual way," she said, with an anxious look.

"It would be, if all married people were like you and me."

She sat for some time, pondering his words. Then, "I don't know," she said, "but it seems to me the old way is a very good one. If I had my—" No, she could not say "widow's third" and maintain her composure. "Tell me," she asked instead, "why you have acted so out of the common. I should like to know your reasons."

"Well, Harriet, I look at it in this way. If I had lived out my natural life, there would n't have been any division of property, and I can't see why matters should n't rest just as they are. It 's partly on your account," he went on, "and still more on account of the children. You 've always been the best judge of what was good for them. Besides," he added, after a few more words of explanation, "I 've been in the habit of considering that the money was as much yours as mine."

Again he paused, and Harriet did not break the silence. Later, when the early dusk was in the chamber, he said, "You and I have always been very united, Harriet."

He held out his hand to her. She took it in both hers.

"Dear girl!" he whispered.

If she had been of a brooding nature she would have taken a mournful pleasure ever after in the pattering rain upon the tin roof. But she was indulgent neither to herself nor to others, and as she entered upon her widowhood she deliberately composed her mind to a calm acquiescence, which, like the shingled roof, gave forth the least possible vibration to reminders of her sorrow.

Her four sons and her two married daughters had all escaped the quicksands of youth, and were now well launched upon their several careers. She could not but take pride in her successful guidance, to which she justly attributed a share in this happy consummation. She had now but one child remaining with her in her spacious house, the "little Lucy," as she still was called, a good, obedient girl of eighteen, who had never given her mother a moment's trouble. Hers was a figure that was rarely present to her mother's mind during the anxious vigils which that responsible woman kept. Hers was the name least often mentioned in her mother's prayers; for Harriet was, in her way, a religious woman. She was not as zealous a church member as one would have expected so active and capable a woman to be. Indeed, her own affairs might well absorb her energies. But her private devotions were none the less earnest. She did much of what her mother once called "thinking on her knees." She was sometimes vaguely aware, after a longer maintenance of this attitude than was usual, that she had been silently talking things over rather than offering praise or supplication. Yet these prolonged statements of her case before a perfect Intelligence often brought her to a better understanding of her own needs and her own best course than she could otherwise have reached. If her religious rites lacked piety, they were at least alive with conscience. And though all her children were remembered in these secret communings, little Lucy's name was so unsuggestive of perplexities that it rarely received more than a passing mention.

One brilliant winter's day Lucy came down stairs arrayed in her squirrel tippet and muff, and wearing a little squirrel cap which sat jauntily on her bright brown hair. She had a fine color, and as she stopped at the sitting-room door to say that she was going over to see Grandma and Aunt Betsy, her mother was struck by her good looks. Indeed, so pleasant was the impression she received that Harriet, usually rather unsusceptible to merely "skin-deep" charms, got up from her chair, and still holding her sewing in her hand, stepped to the window to look out. Lucy lingered for a moment at the top of the long flight of stone steps, down which she then passed with a pretty, swaying motion all her own. "Little Lucy" had a good height, and was in other respects more like her mother than any one had yet discovered. As she reached the driveway below she turned abruptly, with a remarkably bright smile, and bowed. Following the direction of her glance, her mother beheld a surprising apparition. At the side gate stood a young man wearing a corduroy jacket, and holding in his hand a broader-brimmed hat than was then the fashion. His close cropped head thus exposed was a particularly shapely one, though that good point was lost upon his sharp-eyed observer. She meanwhile could see that he was speaking, and if it had not been for Lucy's expressive face she would have supposed that he was a stranger inquiring his way. What, then, was her astonishment when the smiling Lucy went toward the side gate, greeted the still hatless individual with outstretched hand, and, turning, walked away with him in the opposite direction from "Grandma's." Harriet found herself supplied with food for reflection which occupied her the rest of the morning.

Shortly before dinner the truant Lucy appeared, looking flushed and happy, and unmindful of her mother's stern countenance, proceeded to take off her gloves and loosen her tippet. Harriet, apparently intent upon her seam, sewed steadily on, waiting for the child to speak.

"I did n't go to Grandma's after all," said Lucy, stepping to the front window and gazing in an absorbed way across the snow.

Harriet stopped her sewing and looked up, expectant.

"Where did you go?" she asked.

" I went to walk with Frank Enderby. We walked away out into the country and it was perfectly glorious."

The girl had turned her glowing face toward her mother.

" Frank Enderby ! " Harriet repeated, with increased displeasure. " Was that Italian-looking m⌐n, waiting for you at the gate, Frank Enderby ? "

" Why, yes ! Did you see him ? And did n't you know him ? "

" I never thought of such a thing. When did he come back ? "

" The 14th of last month," said Lucy, with prompt exactitude.

" And have you seen much of him ? "

" I 've seen him three times, not counting to-day."

" Where have you been seeing him ? "

" The first time was at Annie Owen's party. And then I saw him at church the next Sunday ; and yesterday he was calling at Annie's when I was there."

" Why did n't you mention him to me ? "

" I don't know," said Lucy, promptly taking refuge in a time-honored subterfuge.

" You must at least know that you were behaving very improperly, when you took a long walk with a young man I 'm not acquainted with."

" I know, Mother ; but I really did n't mean to. He asked me if he might not walk with me to

Grandma's, by way of the common, and before we knew it we were going down Elm Street. You have no idea," she continued, with renewed animation, "how lovely the bare branches of the trees were against the sky. I had never noticed them so much myself, till Frank pointed them out to me. He said it was the best lesson in architecture a man could have, just to see how they met and divided. Do you know, mother, if I were a man, I should have been an architect myself."

"But you 're not a man, Lucy; and I don't like the familiar way in which you are speaking of a perfect stranger."

"But, Mother, Frank is n't a stranger. I 've known him all my life. He used to be ever so good to me when I was a little girl. I was always fond of Frank."

"That was when he was a boy, Lucy. You don't know anything about him since he has grown up. We don't any of us know how he has spent his time in all these years."

"Oh ! but I know. He has been studying like a tiger; he told me so himself. And now he is prepared to build theatres, and cathedrals, and— and houses, and make a great name for himself."

"He 's got a pretty poor one to start with," cried Harriet, with asperity.

"Theatres and cathedrals," she reflected, as Lucy left the room, scarcely heeding her mother's last remark; "theatres and cathedrals, indeed !

Just what I should have expected of him! I should n't be at all surprised if he had turned Romanist. Like as not he was hand in glove with all the play-actors in Europe."

This highly colored view of the young man's probable career was due partly to her profound disapproval of all his antecedents, and partly to his "theatrical" appearance. None of the Dunbridge young men wore velvet jackets and broad-brimmed hats, nor did they stand bareheaded while they talked to a little chit like Lucy. Much as ever if they showed Old Lady Pratt herself such deference. To say nothing of his hair, cropped as close as a jail-bird's! A horrible suspicion crossed Harriet's mind. Could he have been in jail?

It was easy to believe anything, however bad, of a son of Frank Enderby. Had not the father drunk himself into the grave, lingering by the way, however, to drink up a decent fortune? Had not his wife been an inefficient, slatternly woman, without backbone enough to keep her children out of rags? What could one expect of the son of such people? The other children had all died. It was more than likely that the inherited vices of the whole family had centred in this boy. And what was he, after all, but a charity boy, supported, ever since his parents' death, by a rich stranger? A self-respecting young fellow would have gone into a store, and worked his way up. But that was not a fine enough career for Frank Enderby's son. He must needs be "educated" for an architect, and fritter away years of his life in Europe, living the while on charity. An architect, indeed! Nothing but a new fangled name for builder. Had not her own father built half the houses in Dunbridge? Good enough houses for anybody to live in. The stately roof over her own head was a lasting monument to Anson Pratt's skill and ability. Anson Pratt's education had consisted in several years of hard work and privation, as a 'prentice boy. And here was this young upstart requiring all Europe to his teacher! It was just the sort of thing that Harriet had no patience with, and she resolved then and there that this would-be builder of Catholic cathedrals should have no countenance from her family.

But Harriet Spencer was reckoning without "little Lucy," as she might have known at first sight of Lucy's preoccupied face at dinner, and "little Lucy," up to this time, was practically an unknown factor even to her mother.

One of Old Lady Pratt's many wise sayings was, "There's nothin' more likely to come to pass than what you ain't lookin' for." Holding which view, she should have been proof against surprise.

Now it surely would have been difficult to imagine anything more in accordance with this philosophy than Lucy's sudden elevation to inconvenient prominence in the family councils. And

yet so inconsistent is even the wisest philosopher
that when Harriet, a few weeks later, unfolded
to her mother this new and growing perplexity,
Old Lady Pratt so far forgot herself as to lay down
her knitting, take off her steel-bowed spectacles,
and exclaim : " Well, I never ! That beats me,
I declare for 't !' "

They were in Old Lady Pratt's sunny sitting-
room, with the pretty green three-ply carpet on
the floor, and the canary bird singing lustily
above the plants in the window. Deaf Aunt
Betsy was sitting by, nodding her head over her
worsted-work, but she was no interruption to
confidences. If she marked the agitation which
caused her mother to take off her spectacles, she
gave no sign. Betsy rarely knew the preliminary
intricacies of the family affairs. She was thought
to have had her share of the excitement if she
received sufficient warning to enable her to get a
sofa cushion worked in time for the wedding.
So, when she observed her mother's withered fingers tightly holding the bows of the shining spectacles—careful even in her excitement that the
glasses should not get blurred—Betsy merely took
a critical survey of her worsteds, and choosing a
rich green, proceeded to fill in one of her " heart
patterns " with it, rejoicing in the fine contrast it
offered to its brilliant crimson neighbor.

" And you feel sure, Harriet, that it ain't jest a
passing fancy ? "

" I 'm afraid it 's more 'n that, Mother. Lucy
has n't been the same girl since I took her to task

about it. She used to be the *evenest* of all my children, and now she 's either moping about from morning till night, or else she 's as high-flying as a long-tail kite. I thought first myself that she 'd see the sense of what I said to her, and I did n't believe she 'd mind breakin' with him after such a short acquaintance. That 's why I made up my mind not to say anything to you about it. I knew just how you 'd feel about Frank Enderby's son, and how you 'd hate——"

"Fudge, Harriet! 'T ain't Frank Enderby I object to. Frank would ha' come out straight enough if he 'd had any kind of a wife. It 's Frank's wife I never could abide—a weak, shiftless, wishy-washy woman! It always did rile me jest to *look* at Sally Enderby; and I must say 't would put me out more 'n most anything I can think of to have any of my own kith and kin on more 'n speakin' terms with a child of hers."

"But, Mother, Frank Enderby was a drunkard," Harriet remonstrated.

"I don't care 'f he was. Any man with a spark of sperit would have gone to the dogs with such a wife as that."

Harriet gave a little gasp of consternation.

"Well," she said, when she had recovered herself sufficiently to speak, "I never thought I should live to hear you stand up for a drunkard!"

The old lady gave her a shrewd look, and a gleam of humor came into the bright old eyes— Harriet did take things so seriously.

" You 'll have to hear a good many surprising things before you 're as old as I be," she answered, tranquilly resuming her spectacles and her knitting-work.

The canary, as though startled by his old friend's heresy, had fallen into a sudden silence. For a little while the click of the knitting-needles and Betsy's soft woolly manipulations were the only sounds audible.

Then Old Lady Pratt said : " How would it do to send Lucy away on a visit? May be Jane could have her at her house for a spell."

Jane was a daughter of the house of Pratt who had married somewhat " beneath her." She lived in a smoky manufacturing town about ten miles distant from the genteel suburb where the Pratts "resided." Her husband was an optician in a small way, who had not made a success of life, and one would have supposed that there was not much in the nature of festivity to be enjoyed in Jane's stuffy little house. But there was a theory in the Pratt family that a visit must necessarily be considered as an indulgence, and Harriet answered, with decision :

" No, Mother, I 've no idea of humorin' her ; she don't deserve it. And besides," she added, " it is n't likely 't would do any good. You know it was just what you tried with Jane herself, and after all she married Henry Bennett before the year was out."

" We 'll let by-gones be by-gones," said Old

Lady Pratt, rather sharply. She had been "disapp'inted" in Jane's marriage, but she did not propose to cry over spilt milk.

Little Lucy, meanwhile, was having a hard time. Her mother's disapproval was no light affliction, living, as she did, alone with her in that big house, with nobody else to speak to. Harriet had never been a demonstrative mother. She had a certain manner under which she concealed her affection for her children as carefully as she concealed her abundant gray hair beneath a false front. Overt tenderness was not the fashion of the day, nor would it have accorded well with Harriet's self-contained temperament. But though Lucy missed no accustomed warmth, she felt an unaccustomed chill, and it was hard to bear; the more so, as she had gained little in the way of compensation. She "liked" Frank Enderby, and she modestly "hoped" that he liked her. Even in her inmost thoughts Lucy never used a warmer word. Yes, she liked him, and he was very "nice" to her; and how could she break with him as her mother wished her to do? She never thought of disobeying her mother; that was quite out of the question. But, oh! it was very hard.

"I might as well be a nun, and never go anywhere," she had said, in a melancholy little voice, when her mother had carefully laid down the law as to her conduct.

A new look of displeasure had appeared in

Harriet's severe face, but she said nothing. She only made a mental note of the little speech as being "another foreign notion."

To-day, while her mother was "gone to Grandma's," Lucy stood at a front window, gazing idly across the snow-covered lawn to the street, as young girls will gaze when the house seems e.npty, and the outside world is full of possibilities. She told herself she was hoping that Annie Owen might come to see her.

Suddenly she beheld her pet kitten, a frisky little bunch of gray fur, scurrying across the snow toward the street, toward all the dangers that menace little kittens in this wicked world. Quick as thought, Lucy had snatched her Red Riding-hood cape, that was hanging on the hat-tree, and was running swiftly toward the "evergreen corner" in pursuit. She found kitty examining with much interest the shady recesses beneath a dark hemlock, whose branches swept the ground. Puss paid no heed to her mistress' voice. She was stepping daintily about in the snow, lifting her soft little paws very high, and evincing great surprise when her waving tail brought a sudden shower of white powder down upon her from the low-hanging needles.

"Here, kitty, kitty! Come, puss, come!" Lucy called, in persuasive tones. But pussy did not move an eyelid in response.

Now Lucy, whose very decided will was trained to submission in several legitimate direc-

HARRIET.

tions, had no mind to be thwarted by her own kitten. She drew her little red cape tightly about her, and diving in among the wet prickly branches, seized Miss Pussy Cat by the back of her neck, and pulled her out. "Bad pussy," she said, in a caressing tone, holding the warm little creature up against her cheek. The red cape and the dark hair were well powdered with snow, but Lucy did not move away directly. It felt warm and sheltered in there among the tall dark hemlocks, with a blue sky for a roof. She stood, lost in a sudden girlish reverie, softly stroking the kitten, which purred contentedly against her chin.

"I wish you liked me half as well as you do that kitten, Lucy," said a voice she knew.

The sidewalk was close at hand, with only a low stone wall between. He stood holding the branches of the evergreens apart, and looking in upon her with a deprecating, beseeching face. It seemed like a part of her reverie, his coming had been so silent. She did not more than half believe it was really he. She looked at him incredulously for an instant, and then, still gazing into his ardent eyes, she said: "Oh, Frank, I do, I do!"

Before he could speak or look an answer, she had turned and fled across the snow.

But she could not flee so lightly the echo of her own daring words, and all that day and evening the impulse of flight was still strong upon her.

At last, when bedtime came, Lucy said to her mother, "I wish you would let me go to Aunt Jane's for a visit."

Her eyes were fixed upon the carpet. Her mother thought they looked swollen and red.

"Why do you want to go to Aunt Jane's?"

"I should like to get away from home."

"Why?"

She lifted her eyes to her mother's. Mother and daughter were very much alike at that moment.

"Why?" Harriet repeated.

"It is n't easy to do as you wish me to at home, and——"

"And what?"

"I should like to think it over quietly."

There was no defiance in the tone. It seemed to Harriet as though she were listening to her own voice. A peculiar sense of identity with the girl came over her, and she did not resent the speech. If Lucy really did resemble her in character there was nothing to fear. Harriet, with all her determination, would never have rebelled against lawful authority.

"Go to bed now, child," she said, not unkindly; "I will think about it."

When she left Lucy at her Aunt Jane's the next day, with no more enlivening companionship than that of her dull old bachelor cousin, Anson Bennett, Harriet felt some misgivings.

"I don't know 's it 's just the place for her,"

she said to herself. "If she wants to fret and pine, there 's nothing at Jane's to hinder."

For the moment she felt out of humor with herself, and mistrustful of her own wisdom. But this dissatisfaction soon gave place to the much less irksome feeling of annoyance with others. For during Lucy's three weeks' absence, her mother heard so much of young Frank Enderby that she got into a state of chronic displeasure against the world in general. He seemed to have bewitched the neighborhood.

"Just like his father," she would say to herself, rocking so fiercely that she could not sew. "Frank Enderby always had a taking way with him. These good-for-nothing fellows are very apt to."

She felt more determined than ever in her opposition to him. But still his praises resounded. He was going to be a great architect. He had set up an office of his own in the city. He was already paying off the debt to his rich benefactor. It was rumored that he was to have the building of the new Episcopal church in Dunbridge, and that there were to be stained-glass windows in it, and two pulpits. As time went on Harriet began to feel that the whole community was in league against her, and she summoned all her will and diplomacy to avert the crisis which she feared.

One day Old Lady Pratt was passing the afternoon with her daughter. The two women had established themselves comfortably over the iron register, whence issued a mild, well-regulated heat, very pleasing to a well-regulated mind. They talked amicably of this and that, while their knitting-needles clicked accompaniment, and Harriet had begun to feel more at one with herself and with the world at large than had been the case for some time past. Suddenly, as out of a clear sky, the old lady remarked:

" 'T ain't often that you see a handsomer house than this, Harriet."

Now the superiority of the Spencer house over others of the neighborhood was an established fact, and one that hardly called for comment at this late day. Harriet could not but wonder at the turn her mother's thoughts had taken. She soon caught their drift, however.

"I must say," the latter continued, "that I was quite pleased to hear that young Enderby has been heard to say that 'Old Anson Pratt's houses' were a long sight ahead of the new 'French-roof monstrosities.' He called 'em *mon-strosities*, Harriet," she repeated, with a quiet chuckle.

Harriet's face suddenly hardened. "I always thought the French-roof houses very pretty myself," said she.

Her mother glanced at her quickly.

"I hope you ain't so sot agin that boy as you was, Harriet. Far 's I can make out, he seems to be a likely enough young fellow."

"Likely enough to go to the bad," Harriet retorted, sharply.

"He ain't showed no signs of it yet," the old lady rejoined, with answering spirit. "He 'pears to be doin' uncommon well. Dr. Baxter says he 's makin' his mark a'ready."

"He has n't stopped being the son of his father and mother, far 's I know."

"That 's true enough, and I never could abide Sally Enderby. But then, folks don't always take after their fathers and mothers."

"I don't know who else they take after," cried Harriet, with as near an approach to irritability as she ever permitted herself. "Anyway, my mind 's made up about Lucy. She sha' n't have anything to do with Frank Enderby, not if I have to *lock her up*."

Old Lady Pratt eyed her daughter an instant. It was one of the rare occasions on which she was displeased with her.

"Speakin' of takin' after your parents," she said, dryly, "you ain't one mite like your father."

The reproof was administered, and the culprit knew it.

Opposition is a great stiffener. From that time forward Harriet Spencer's determination had turned to obstinacy.

When Lucy came home a few days later, her mother, after a searching glance at her pale face, gave her a rather frosty greeting. The girl wore a deep red rose in her dress.

4

"Where did you get that rose?" Harriet asked presently, for hot-house flowers did not bloom at Jane's.

"Frank left it for me yesterday."

"Did he come 'way over to Westville on purpose to see you?"

"I don't know."

"How did he find out you were at Jane's?"

"I don't know."

"Did n't you ask him?"

"I did n't see him."

"Why not?"

"I thought it would be mean."

The inquisitor's face relaxed.

"Did Jane see him?"

"Yes 'm."

"What did she say to him?"

"I don't know. She said she made it all right."

"Jane had better mind her own business," Harriet muttered.

She was suspicious of her sister's methods. Jane's had never been a well-regulated mind. But the rose was suffered to remain where it was. Lucy had certainly behaved very well, exactly as Harriet herself would have done in her place.

When she said good-night, Lucy still looked pale and tired; but there was a "grown-up," experienced look in her face which did not escape her mother.

Harriet was again struck with that curious sense of identity with her which had come over

her once before. " I guess it 's that red rose," she
said to herself, with a dreary feeling at her heart.

Harriet's devotions that evening were serious
and absorbing. Long after the house was quiet
she still knelt beside her bed, her head resting in
her hands. Yet meek as was the attitude, her
face, when she lifted it, was harder than before;
the set look seemed fixed there. She put out her
light and got into bed, but she could not compose
herself to sleep. Hour after hour she lay with her
eyes wide open, staring into the darkness. She
had ceased to think; she had ceased to resolve.
She was trying, with a dull, persistent effort, not
to see that red rose and the pale face above it, so
like her own. The tall clock in the dining-room
struck eleven and twelve. Then the minutes
dragged so slowly that she hoped she had been
asleep. But no; the next stroke that echoed
through the empty halls was one. At two o'clock
something seemed to give way within her. She
got up and struck a light, and having put on her
heavy flannel double-gown and slippers, she
stood for a moment irresolute. She glanced furtively at the old mahogany bureau between the
front windows, and then, candle in hand, she
passed out into the warm hall and down the
stairs. As the old timbers creaked beneath her
feet she paused, and cast a guilty look over her
shoulder. "If this is n't perfectly ridiculous!"
she said to herself, with strong disapproval. But
she pursued her way still more cautiously.

Arrived below she went about from room to room feeling the window fastenings. Yet she had secured them all herself, and Harriet Spencer was the last woman to doubt her own thoroughness. The long parlor was dim and shadowy in the flickering candle-light, and her own figure seen in the pier-glass as she came down the room had a ghostly look. She turned her eyes away from the glass, and was glad to go out into the hall.

In the kitchen she examined the bread, which had been set to rise. It was doing its duty bravely. The gray kitten, curled up in its little basket beside the stove, opened one eye upon the intruder, but it told no tales of hemlock boughs and Red Riding-hood capes, nor of a swift passage across the snow, held close against a wildly beating heart.

A few moments later Harriet was standing at Lucy's bedside. The girl was fast asleep, but the candle-light upon her face showed it flushed and tear-stained. In the mug upon the washstand the red rose drooped its head. Harriet bent down and breathed the delicate perfume, shading the candle lest the light should wake the sleeper. "I wish I could sleep like that," she thought, sighing deeply. "'T is n't much of a trouble that don't keep you awake nights."

Yet the touch was very gentle with which she drew the warm coverlid closer about the child.

Harriet was not herself to-night. For once in her life she had slipped from her own guidance. Something from without seemed to direct her movements; or was it something deep, deep within? As she closed her chamber door and put the candle upon the bureau, she made one last, half-hearted effort to break the spell which was upon her, but the effort was vain. A look of unwonted emotion transformed her handsome features, and, in sudden defiance of her own will, she pulled open a certain bureau drawer, and reaching far back under the cool linen, drew forth an old shell box. Her hands trembled a little as she lifted the lid. The subtle odor which clings about old letters floated up. She took them out and opened them, one after the other, straining her eyes to read them in the uncertain candle-light. Curiously enough, she did not think of putting on her glasses. The young eyes for which those lines were written had required no such aids. Each letter began: "My beloved Harriet," and each one was signed: "Your faithful James." Nor did they differ very greatly in their contents, these three or four yellow letters with the ink fading out. She read them slowly and with difficulty, a deep crimson coming into her cheeks, a strange softness into her eyes.

Last of all, she took up a piece of silk tissue-paper lying folded together in the bottom of the box. How long it was since she had looked at it! The creases were worn quite through. Lying

within,—yes, there it was, a faded rose, no longer
red. The dull brownish petals would have
crumbled had her touch been less tender. For a
long, long time she looked at it before laying it
carefully back into the box ; then, with a sudden,
passionate movement, she bowed her gray head
upon the open letters, and wept—wept not like an
old woman, but like a young girl in an abandon-
ment of grief.

The candle burnt lower and lower, while Harriet Spencer sat and wept ; the old clock struck
three, and the faint yet pervasive odor of the
yellowing paper crept slowly through the quiet
chamber. It was gray dawn before the weary
watcher sank into a troubled sleep.

But that short sleep bridged the way back to
real life. There was no trace of weariness in the
brisk step with which Harriet went about the
house the next morning. Her voice, too, was
quite steady and matter-of-fact as she said to
Lucy : "How would you like to have me send
and ask Frank Enderby to come in to supper
to-night, seeing he was so polite as to go 'way
over to Jane's to wait on you. We are going to
have waffles," she tried to add, but there were
close clinging arms about her neck and a soft cheek
was pressed against her own for answer. Such
behavior did not seem to Harriet quite decorous.
She actually blushed, as she put the girl gently
from her, saying : "There, there, Lucy ! Don't
take on about it."

Little Lucy did not mark the strangely tired look in her mother's eyes. A happy wonder filled her heart, and shut out all besides.

At the wedding, a year or two after that, some one remarked, "How well-preserved Harriet Spencer is!"

"Yes," said the widow Perkins, with a self-conscious sigh; "that comes of keeping your feelings under."

III.

A DOMESTIC CRISIS.

ANSON PRATT the younger was something of an old Betty. His mother had made the discovery when he was still in petticoats, and she had tried by many ingenious devices to change his nature. He was only her second child, and she, being then young and inexperienced, had not yet learned that natures are not to be changed. Years, however, and an instructive family of children taught her wisdom. She brought her son up in the paths of godliness and temperance ; she inculcated in him the most sterling principles ; she taught him self-reliance and integrity. But an old Betty he remained to the end of the chapter.

This was the more unfortunate since he had married a woman who would have seemed especially designed by Providence to be a trial to an old Betty in any capacity, and pre-eminently so in the capacity of helpmeet. Yet there were compensations in his lot, which Anson Pratt would have been the last man to underrate.

Emmeline Joy, though not possessed of beauty, was a woman of a good deal of personal fascination. She had a piquant face and great vivacity. She had also her seasons of dreaminess—of remoteness from every-day concerns. She passed for an accomplished woman in the good old simple days when she was young, before the world grew critical and fault-finding, when people were still easily pleased. She could sing, and play the piano—a queer little thin-voiced instrument, having the maker's name done in mother-of-pearl, with floral ornamentations, on the lid. She could paint in water-colors, to the admiration of all beholders. She had a delightful talent for acting, and she so far succeeded in overcoming the prejudices of the Puritan community into which she had married, as to introduce private theatricals into staid old Dunbridge itself. She did none of these things well, judged by modern standards, unless it was perhaps the acting, in which she really excelled, by virtue of a remarkable power of mimicry and a spontaneity as refreshing as it was unusual. In music and painting she had no more technical facility than many of her contemporaries. But there was a touch of genius in all that she did, which made it go straight to people's hearts. Her painted flowers may have been a trifle out of drawing, but somehow she seemed to have got their fragrance into her pictures. The dear, old-fashioned tunes she played and sang were very primitive, but her touch made them beautiful. And the same spark of genius that prevailed in what she did, also made her what she was, a woman of singular charm and lovableness. It was no wonder that Anson Pratt fell in love with her, in spite of her well known shortcomings ; it was no wonder that he was quite as much in love with her as ever, after having suffered from those shortcomings for seven years.

Emmeline's manifold faults might all be summed up in a word—she was the very worst housekeeper imaginable. Anson Pratt, old Betty as he was, was forced to live in the midst of disorder and dust ; he had to see his two boys, bright little fellows with a capacity for getting into trouble, going about in rags and tatters. He himself had more than once experienced the humiliation of substituting a pin for a button ; he had sometimes walked the streets with the degrading consciousness of a hole in his socks. This would have been hard enough for any man to bear. For an old Betty it was wellnigh intolerable. Furthermore, although he was not an epicure, Anson liked his meals well cooked and well served, and this reasonable wish was rarely gratified. Slatternly, inefficient servants succeeded one another in the kitchen, and unpalatable viands appeared as a result upon the table. Emmeline never seemed to notice what she ate. She had a good, healthy appetite and a preoccupied mind, and she could not understand any one's being fastidious about his food.

To do Anson justice, it was some time before he complained. During the early part of his married life the muddiest coffee had the flavor of nectar when his wife's hands poured it out ; the most unpalatable food of her serving seemed ambrosial. And when, after many months, he returned to a normal state of mind, and ventured upon a mild protest, Emmeline hardly took it in earnest. In fact, Emmeline was the only person who knew Anson Pratt intimately, who had not discovered that he was an old Betty.

Mrs. Anson's general inefficiency was the more aggravating, because it existed side by side with unusual capacity. When, at not very rare intervals, the maid-of-all-work took French leave, Emmeline invariably rose to the occasion. Then it was that Anson was well fed and well cared for. Appetizing dishes were served in the most appetizing manner. The touch of genius which Emmeline possessed, the quick perception and the light hand, made themselves felt in the homeliest tasks on which she really put her mind. The difficulty usually was that she did not put her mind on these things. She had too many bad habits, which interfered with that system so essential in the government of a household. She would read Scott or Byron until far into the night, and wake in the morning dazed and sleepy. Or again, she would rise with the sun and take her boys for a long walk, out into the dewy fields, to listen to the meadow thrush, instead of busying herself with housewifely duties. She had been known to practise an entire morning on a new piano piece, to spend days in fashioning a velvet tunic for Robbie, or an embroidered skirt for little Aleck, while the boys, happily unconscious, shocked the neighborhood in their well ventilated pinafores and tattered hats.

The two boys were very different, even at the age of five and three, respectively. Robbie, the elder, was the greater rogue of the two, the one who took the initiative in every scheme of mischief, leading the small boys of the neighborhood, as well as his matter-of-fact little brother, into scrapes innumerable. Yet when Emmeline played the piano, or sang an old ballad, the little figure that stole in on tiptoe and curled itself up in the corner of the sofa, that sat there motionless as long as the music lasted, was Robbie's, and Robbie's were the little arms that were most often flung about her neck in a burst of passionate affection, or an equally passionate burst of penitence. It was the little Robbie who was improvident with his playthings, who emptied his entire store of pennies for the roughest tramp who came their way. It was little Robbie who gave his mother more trouble and more delight than a dozen little Alecks could have done.

Aleck, on the other hand, was his father's boy, the boy for whom Anson already prophesied success in life, and considering that the two were little Pratts, brought up in Dunbridge, this prophecy was likely enough to come true. The old New England community of half a century ago knew how to prize a level head and a well-governed mind. Genius and impetuosity were rather thrown away upon our forebears. A boy who drew pictures on his slate instead of doing his sums, who forgot his history dates in enthusiasm over the history heroes, did not, in old times, arouse the tender and peculiar interest of his teachers. Nobody but his mother looked upon Robbie as anything more than a bright but troublesome little lad, with ears in crying need of being boxed.

Meanwhile, Emmeline lived an abstracted sort of life, throwing herself ardently into whatever happened to appeal to her for the moment, adoring her husband and her little boys, and taking the worst possible care of them. She led her own life of the imagination and the emotions, curiously oblivious of the clouds that were gathering on the domestic horizon. And Anson, tired of protesting, tired of "putting up" with things, tired of living "out at elbows," was gradually forming a great resolve.

For several weeks past, Emmeline had been given over, heart and soul, to the preparations for a "parlor comedy," to be performed in aid of a fund for buying a new church organ. She had not only to play the title-rôle, "The Artless Celestina," but she was stage-manager as well.

This latter undertaking was the more arduous
of the two, because of the uncompromising stiff-
ness of the material she had to work with. The
women of her little troupe, sensible wives and
daughters of Dunbridge citizens, women who
had all their lives been engaged in repressing
their more lively emotions, in refraining from
indecorous exhibitions of feeling, found it difficult
to teach their voices the art of trembling, their
features the trick of looking moved in an imagi-
nary situation. The estimable youth who had
assumed the rôle of insinuating villain could
scarcely be induced not to state his designs and
convey the subtle cunning of his machinations in
a voice with which he might have taken command of an army. As to Celestina's lover,
though his declaration of undying affection
smacked strongly of the counting-house, his arms
and legs would have done credit to a Dutch
windmill. But Emmeline never for a moment
lost heart. She drilled her unpromising company with tact and spirit, and she threw into her
own rôle a naturalness and fire which held its
own against all odds. The play, according to
Dunbridge standards, turned out a success, and
the "leading lady" went home with her husband
after the performance, exhausted but triumphant.

But great as had been Emmeline's perplexities,
this period of excitement and anxiety had been far
more severe a strain upon Anson's nerves than
upon hers. His house had been more at sixes

and sevens than ever, his children had taken on more than ever the semblance of street-ragamuffins, and as for his food, he was left to the mercy of the most inefficient servant who had yet dispensed indigestion to this long-suffering household.

Yet Anson possessed himself in patience all through the time of rehearsals. He was even magnanimous enough to take a pride in his wife's success. He was a little bewildered, indeed, by the ease and naturalness with which she played the part of designing coquette, but her eagerness, when she turned to her rightful lord for approval, once the play being ended, proved entirely reassuring.

The next day Anson laid before her his list of grievances, and waited in the lingering hope of better things. Alas! It was a vain hope. Emmeline took his fault-finding in the sweetest spirit, promised to " see to things," and to " speak to " the servant, and immediately became absorbed in the manufacture of a pair of slippers for her husband's birthday, and forgot all about everything else.

Anson felt deeply injured, as he certainly had a right to do. He thought bitterly of his own hardworking life, of how he never looked to the right nor to the left when in the path of duty, of the discomforts and vexations he had endured for all these years, and his heart became hard within him.

On the evening of the third day after the theatricals he went down cellar to saw wood, a favorite diversion of his. He liked the damp, cold, clean cellar, and the sense of having his own way in his own province; he liked to feel his hand close firmly upon the smooth handle of the saw, he enjoyed the tingling sensation that went through the sole of his foot, pressed hard against the log, as the saw ground its way through the resisting fibres of the wood. On a cold March evening like this the exercise was particularly agreeable.

To-night, however, his mind was laboring harder than his muscles. Yes, he thought to himself,—sawing wood is rough work, and it makes a grating sound. But some difficulties have to be sawed through in just that hard, uncompromising way. As he tossed one stick after another onto the pile, he first held it in the small circle of light his lantern cast, and admired the smooth, even cut which the ugly tool had made. And as he worked, and as he pondered, he experienced a strong desire to saw through the difficulties of his daily life, no matter how rude and jarring the process might be.

He had a right to have a comfortable home, if ever a man had. It was a right that he fairly earned, every day of his life. Emmeline was very sweet, and he loved her very much, but, good heavens! a man could not live on sweetness and love! He kept sawing one log after another to the required length, and when he had had enough of it, he drew himself up, and took a long breath.

" I 'll do it ! " he said to himself ; " I swear I 'll do it."

" It 'll cost a good deal," he continued, as he put on his coat and hung up his saw on its own special peg, "but I can make it up somehow."

He went up stairs into the kitchen, where he hung up his lantern, and washed his hands at the sink. Then, as he passed on into the front of the house, he heard Emmeline's voice, singing a lullaby in the nursery. He paused and listened. Emmeline's singing always appealed to him. To-night her voice was wonderfully sweet, and he liked the words :

"Father 's a nobleman, mother 's a queen."

Emmeline made her own tunes when she sang to the children. The melody was low and crooning, and in the middle of it Anson could hear little Robbie's voice, saying sleepily : " Kiss me again, Mamma."

Anson leaned against the balustrade.

"Father 's a nobleman, mother 's a queen."

Was father a nobleman, to care so much about sordid things? Was not Emmeline, after all, a kind of queen, not made for common cares?

"Father 's a nobleman, mother 's a queen."

She had left out the rest of the verse now, and was merely murmuring that one line. For the hundredth time Anson Pratt's heart softened, and

5

his annoyances seemed petty and unreal. He took his hand off the railing, meaning to go up to the nursery, when his eye fell upon a long streak of dust, that ran over his hand, his wristband, and his coat-sleeve. He shuddered at the sight of it as only an old Betty could do, and striding into the sitting-room he slammed the door behind him.

The rude sound startled Emmeline out of her reverie, and little Aleck waked up crying.

The next evening, after the children were put to bed, Emmeline came down to the sitting-room, looking very pretty and housewifely in a black silk apron, with a white muslin neckerchief crossed over her breast. She took a good deal of pride in looking matronly, and longed for the time when Anson would let her wear a cap. Her face fell as she saw that her husband was reading his paper by the aid of a very smoky lamp.

"Oh, Anson," she cried, "I 'm so sorry! I shall have to get you another lamp."

"Can't the girl fill this one?" he asked.

Anson had long since given up trying to keep run of the "girls'" names.

"I 'm afraid there is n't any oil," she said, regretfully; "but never mind, the other lamp will do to talk by."

"Yes, any light will do to talk by." When the change had been made, Emmeline came and sat down beside him, with her little confiding air, which had disarmed him more than once when he was on the verge of rebellion. But this time his heart was steeled.

Anson Pratt was a fine-looking man, an advantage of which he himself made very little account. If he had been told that he had more actual beauty than his wife, he would have been much offended. It was nevertheless a fact, and one which Emmeline knew and gloried in. To-night as she glanced at his handsome face in the half-light cast by the second-best lamp, a sudden misgiving seized her. The face was not at its best. The finely marked brows were contracted, the eyes looked nearer together than was quite becoming, the lips were so tightly compressed as to seem thinner than usual. Decidedly, Anson was out of sorts. Oh! what was it this time? Was it buttons? Or was it fat in the gravy? or——''

"Emmeline," Anson said, in a slightly constrained voice, "I have been making up my mind about something for a long time, and now my mind is made up."

This was evidently a more serious matter than buttons or gravy, and Emmeline's courage revived, as it had a way of doing in the face of a real trouble.

"What is it, Anson? Do you think you 'll have to take a partner after all?"

"Something like it," he answered, avoiding her eyes as he spoke. "I 've engaged a house-keeper."

"A what?"

"A housekeeper."

"Engaged a housekeeper? Why, Anson, what do you mean!"

"I mean exactly what I say. I 've engaged the woman Sister Harriet was telling us about. She 's coming to-morrow afternoon."

"Coming here, to keep house for you? To take my place?"

"She 's coming here to keep this house." Emmeline had grown very white.

"Why have you taken such a step without consulting me?"

"Because I was sure you would object, and I did n't want any discussion."

"But, Anson, what do you want of a house-keeper?"

"What most folks want of a housekeeper. To have the house kept." Anson was desperately afraid that his wife would persuade him to abandon his plan, and before she could interpose he had armed himself from top to toe in his grievances.

"I have borne a great deal, Emmeline. I 've lived for seven years without any of the comforts of a home. There is n't a man in Dunbridge who has had so much to put up with as I. And I 've made up my mind that I 'm not going to stand it another day. I 'm going to try for once what it is like to have a clean house and whole clothes and something fit to eat."

"You 've lived for seven years without the comforts of a home ? Do you mean that, Anson ? "

"I mean just that."

"And there is n't a man in Dunbridge who has been so badly off as you ? "

"In some respects, no ! There is n't a man in Dunbridge that is as badly off as I."

Emmeline got up from her chair and walked about the room with swift, nervous movements. Anson kept his seat and kept his determination.

At last Emmeline came back and knelt down beside his chair.

There were very few women of her day and generation who could have knelt down in just that supplicating way, and very few voices that could have sounded so beseeching as did hers.

"Anson, won't you please give me one more trial? Won't you please tell that woman not to come ? "

"No, I won't," he answered stolidly. "I 've made up my mind to have a little comfort, and I 've engaged Mrs. Beach for a month, beginning to-morrow."

"But, Anson, for my sake, for both our sakes, tell her not to come. Oh, Anson ! I cannot bear it ! I am sure I cannot bear it—please—please don't let her come."

Her tone of passionate entreaty was too intense to move him. It seemed to him like play acting.

"I tell you, Emmeline," he said, getting up and leaving her kneeling there beside his chair, "the thing is done, and I 'm not going to undo it. It 's no more than my right to have at least a month's comfort, and I 'm going to have it."

He felt that in saying "at least a month," he had made a great concession.

As he turned away Emmeline got up from her knees and steadied herself against the back of the chair. The blood had rushed back into her white cheeks, and her eyes had an unnatural light in them. But she spoke with a great deal of self-command.

"Anson," she said, and he turned and looked at her. "Anson, you will have to choose between us—I will not stay with you one hour after that woman comes into the house."

"And where shall you go?"

"I don't know. I suppose to mother's. But that is of no consequence. As long as I cannot be your housekeeper, you will have to choose. You can have your new housekeeper, or you can have me, but you can't have both. Oh, Anson, please don't drive me out of the house like this," she cried, coming toward him and putting both hands on his arm.

He remembered the streak of dust that had been there the evening before.

"Nonsense, Emmeline," he said, impatiently, shaking off her hands. "Don't be so theatrical. I 've engaged the woman, and she 's coming, and that 's all there is about it. If you 've a mind to fly into a passion, I can't help it. Only one thing

I must insist upon!'' he added, sharply. "That you stay in your own house where you belong.''

" Nevertheless I shall go.''

There was a tone of quiet self-assertion in her voice that Anson had never heard before, and he suddenly felt himself in a white heat of anger.

" I forbid you to leave the house!'' he cried. His masterful tone was also new to her, and for a moment husband and wife looked at each other, estranged and bewildered, as though all their old moorings had been swept away.

Then Emmeline left him and went slowly up stairs, with despair in her heart. If he could speak to her like that everything was at an end. Oh! Where should she turn, what should she do?

The nursery-door stood open at the head of the stairs, and instinctively she stayed her foot. The children! Neither of them had thought of the children. She went in and closed the door behind her and then she knelt down by the bed and burst into tears.

Tears have been a good deal maligned, but they are a great comfort. While Emmeline wept by the side of her sleeping boy's she got her balance. It was impossible that she should do full justice to Anson's cause of complaint, that she should quite appreciate the enormity of her own transgressions. Indeed, her mind did not busy itself with either the one or the other. She simply struggled to adjust herself to the situation as it existed. After all everything was not over.

Here, at least, in those sturdy little fellows that needed her and needed their father too, was something real and abiding, something of a good deal more importance than anybody's injured sensibilities. No, all was not over. There was nothing to be tragical about. She was wounded, humiliated. It was very grievous. But they would get the better of it yet. Her soul revolted at the thought of the woman who was coming to usurp her place, her soul revolted at the tone in which her husband had spoken to her. But all would yet be well. She was sure that all would yet be well. She kissed the boys very tenderly, and then she slipped into her own room, where she went into consultation with herself.

Anson, meanwhile, resumed his seat and tried hard not to feel like a brute. Men are at a great disadvantage in their quarrels with women. The consciousness of a heavy hand, so to speak, discomposes them. Anson knew very well that in his desperate effort not to soften, he had hardened. He knew that his tone had been masterful, his behavior unchivalrous. Somehow that interview had given him a new and far from agreeable impression of himself. He found himself wondering whether, if he had married a less captivating and irresistible woman than Emmeline, he might not have turned out to be a domestic tyrant. He had always despised domestic tyrants.

Impatiently he sought refuge in the evening paper. But, alas! the print was bad, and the second-best lamp was worse, and this small annoyance restored his wavering resolution.

In the broad light of day matters did not seem quite so serious, and even when Emmeline told him at breakfast that she was really going to pay a visit to her mother, it seemed a sufficiently natural thing to do, and he was relieved to find that it was not worth while to oppose her. Mrs. Joy lived in the city, and her house was easily accessible. He was only surprised that Emmeline did not propose taking the children with her, but he reflected that her mother was in delicate health and might not like two noisy boys about the house.

The "high tragedy" which had annoyed him in Emmeline the evening before had entirely disappeared. Indeed, there was an airy lightness in her manner, when she bade him good-bye, which was mortifying to him. He left the house with rather a heavy, inelastic step, and being but a mortal man, he did not feel her eyes upon him, as she gazed, half-blinded by tears, through the slats of the blinds, after his retreating figure.

And now began the era of peace and order for which Anson Pratt had longed. His new housekeeper proved to be a most efficient woman. She promptly got rid of the kitchen "baggage," as she termed the late incumbent, and took in her place a wild, red-headed Irish girl, freckled to the very tip of her nose, whose astonishing brogue and slam-bang manners made her seem anything but promising. Under Mrs. Beach's skilful generalship, however, she toned down somewhat, and proved to be an admirable servant. Up early in the morning, always busy, cheery, and good-tempered, serving delicious meals, ready to lend a hand with the children, thoughtful, and attentive to her master. She had a way of helping Anson off with his great-coat, and having his slippers in readiness for him, which made him feel like a pampered aristocrat. Nor was he ungrateful.

"Katie," he said to her one evening, "you 're a very good girl. I hope you are contented and happy with us."

"Indade, Sorr, but I *am*," she declared heartily.

"Mrs. Pratt will be pleased to find you here when she comes back."

Anson always made a point of referring to his wife in the presence of Mrs. Beach and Katie, who were quite ready to regard her with respect and admiration. Katie had a queer little way of looking askance when she had anything to say. With her eyes fixed upon Anson's coat-sleeve she asked:

"An' is it long that she 'll be bidin' awa'?"

"No, she will come home before long." Then Katie, blushing violently under her freckles, blurted out: "Beggin' your pardon, Sorr. It 's mesilf as was wonderin' how she could lave your honor and the two swate little boys, at all, at all!"

"Your mistress is obliged to be away," Anson replied, with a dignity which was intentionally chilling to the impulsive Katie. She dropped an apologetic courtesy and retired precipitately to her own domain.

Now Anson Pratt, who had got what he thought he most wanted, namely, an orderly house and a good table,—Anson Pratt, whose buttons were now always sewed on, whose wristbands were never frayed, was, of course, far from happy. Creature comforts are all very well, but they are not in themselves satisfying. Little Robbie quite expressed his father's feelings, when, after the first day of the new régime, Anson took him on his knee and asked him how he liked Mrs. Beach.

"Pretty well," said Robbie, "But I like mamma better."

Anson too found Mrs. Beach and her housekeeping "pretty well," in their way, but with little Robbie he "liked mamma better."

The lamp was always filled now, and he could read his evening paper in comfort. But it was remarkable how often the paper had to wait while he pored over a certain note which he had received the day after Emmeline's departure,—a particularly foolish thing to do, since he knew the note by heart, and could have read it just as well by the light of the second-best lamp, or without any light at all, for the matter of that.

The note had said :

"Dear Anson—

"Mother has asked me to go on a little journey
with her, and as you are so well taken care of I
thought it was a good time to go. . I write this so
that you need not come way up to mother's for
nothing.   I hope you like your new housekeeper
and that you are enjoying all 'the comforts of a
home.'

                    "Your affectionate wife,
                                "Emmeline."

Then there was a short postscript written in a
less careful hand :

"Don't forget me, Anson—and kiss the boys
for me."

Anson did not forget her, though he tried his
best to take her desertion philosophically.   The
evening after Emmeline went away, for instance,
he had resort to his favorite occupation of sawing
wood, and he sawed himself, so to speak, into a
very sensible frame of mind.   But when he came
upstairs and into the front of the house, he
stopped mechanically and listened.   He could
almost hear Emmeline's voice singing :

"Father 's a nobleman, mother 's a queen."

Almost, but not quite.   As he stood with his
hand on the stair railing, his heart sank at the
stillness of the house, and then, lifting his hand,
he involuntarily looked to see if there was any
mark on it.   Singularly enough he experienced

a shock of disappointment. No son or daughter of Old Lady Pratt was ever morbidly sentimental. Yet so much did Anson miss the voice he had listened for, that there would have been consolation, he thought, in the old familiar dirt streak. But alas! nothing was old and familiar. Everything was different.

And even the creature comforts seemed likely to forsake him, for scarcely had Mrs. Beach been in the house a week, when she was suddenly called away by the illness of her daughter.

Anson's heart gave a great bound at the news. Emmeline must come home now. She must come home at once. He would send for her. But where? How? She had given him no address. She had not written to him again. At first he thought he would go to Mrs. Joy's house and find out her whereabouts. But then his pride arose and he said to himself: "She has chosen to leave me in the lurch. She shall choose her own time for coming back."

Happily Katie proved quite equal to the emergency. She was housekeeper and servant in one. She seemed able to look after everything. The house, the kitchen, the master, and the boys.

One evening, soon after Mrs. Beach's departure, Anson went into the sitting-room where he found Katie lighting the lamp. In a glass on the table were the first crocuses of the season. The sight of them touched him. Emmeline had always taken pride in finding the first crocuses as a surprise for him.

He stepped up and looked at them, and at the same time the boys came running in, looking clean and whole as they usually did nowadays. He took little Aleck on his knee, and then he said, as Katie finished her task :

" Did you put those flowers there, Katie ? "

" Yes, Sorr."

She stood, with her apron in her mouth, looking shy and awkward. " I was thinkin', Sorr, as how it seemed so lonesome-like after the childers was put to bed, and I thought as how the shmall flowers might be company for ye'z."

" Thank you, Katie, they are very pretty," said Anson.

" They 's my mamma's flowers," little Robbie declared, looking doubtfully at the smiling Katie. Katie had a grotesque smile. Her lips went down and in at the corners in a manner that was not prepossessing. She fixed her eyes, with an inconsequent expression on the key-board of the piano, and said : " Beggin' your pardon, Sorr, and does the mistress like the flowers ? "

" Yes, Katie. Your mistress likes flowers," Anson replied, with a queer feeling in his throat.

" My mamma 's more beautifuller than those flowers," Robbie asserted stoutly.

Meanwhile little Aleck, who had been rifling his father's pockets, had pulled out a small folded piece of paper. It was before the day of envel-

KATIE.

opes, and as it fell from the child's hand the paper flew open. Katie picked it up and handed it to her master, who folded it carefully, and put it back in his pocket, chiding Aleck rather sharply.

If Katie had been an observing young woman she would have noticed that the bit of paper was a note, much worn, and presumably very old. And yet if she had been quick enough to read the date she would have seen that it was written only ten days ago. But wild Irish girls have not always quick perceptions, and it is hardly to be supposed that Katie made any observations on the subject.

Whatever Katie lacked in perception, however, she made up in feeling. She evidently took her master's lonely and deserted state very much to heart. As she bustled about the dining-room, setting the table for supper, she stopped more than once to dry her eyes on the corner of her apron. Any one observing Katie in her unguarded moments would have discovered that she was one of those unfortunates who are born to do themselves injustice while lavishing devotion upon others. Such an observer would have learned that it was her shyness which distorted her features and made her voice harsh. When she was by herself her freckled face lost much of the gawky look which it took on in the presence of her betters. Her lower jaw did not drop so heavily, her eyes did not look so dull. Her movements, too, were less awkward and jerky as she laid the table in unembarrassed solitude. And when, an hour after supper, she went up to give the boys their baths and put them to bed, there was a tender motherliness about her which was really very winning.

Little Robbie seemed full of thoughts of his mother that evening. He chattered on about her to the sympathetic Katie as she polished off his small pink ears, and even when the ablutions were over his glowing eulogy still continued.

"She's just the most beautifullest lady you ever saw," he declared, as Katie tucked him up in bed beside his little brother. "You'll just love her so! She's got such pretty red cheeks, and such shiny black hair. Katie, don't you wish you was pretty? And she plays the pianner, and she sings, Katie—oh! she sings such pretty songs when she puts us to bed. Can't you sing, Katie? Can't you sing just one little song?"

"Ach! go way wid ye'z!" cried Katie, "and would ye be afther makin' a lady o' the likes o' me?"

She knelt down beside the bed, and tucked the little fellow in, and then she watched him as he fell asleep.

By and by, when he was breathing regularly, the warm flush coming on his cheeks, the lips opening just a trifle, she stooped and kissed him. She laid her arm across him till her hand touched his little brother, and then she began to croon the sweetest song, very, very softly, and strangely enough, the words were the old familiar ones:

"Father 's a nobleman, mother 's a queen."

Robbie stirred in his sleep, and murmured, "Mamma," and she slipped her arm under his head, and he nestled down against her, and she went on singing, singing:

"Father 's a nobleman, mother 's a queen,"

—not quite so softly now.

Anson, sitting down-stairs by himself, with the crocuses beside him, heard the song, and a sudden, superstitious thrill went through him. He dropped his paper, and stole to the foot of the stairs, and the sweet voice, crooning more softly again, just reached his ear.

"Father 's a nobleman, mother 's a queen."

"Emmeline!" he cried, and bounded up the stairs, two steps at a time. There was no light in the nursery, where he could only discern a shadowy figure kneeling by the bed. "Emmeline!" he whispered, "Emmeline!"

"Sh, Anson! Don't wake the children."

He leaned down and tried to lift her up, but, as his eyes grew accustomed to the darkness, he could see little Robbie's head against her breast.

"Emmeline! Emmeline! When did you come home?"

"I 've been here all the time," she said, with

6

a little sob, gently laying Robbie's head upon
the pillow. "You stupid, stupid Anson! You
never knew me!"

"Emmeline! What do you mean?"

"Sure an' I 'm thinkin' the misthress has got
home, Sorr!"

It was the voice of the faithful Katie, whom he
was apparently holding in his arms.

*   *   *   *   *   *

"And did you really think," asked Emmeline,
an hour later, when they sat together by the
light of the best lamp,—"And did you really
think that I could leave you and the children for
ten whole days, and not know how you were
getting along?"

"No, I could n't have thought so," said
Anson, with conviction. "I could n't possibly
have thought that. I must have known all the
time that you were Katie, only I did n't quite
take it in."

As Anson looked at his wife's face, where a
few of the more obdurate freckles still clung, and
into the eyes which looked so natural and so dear,
in spite of the hint of red which still lingered in
the eyebrows, he thought that he had never been
so well content in all his life—no, not even seven
years ago, when his wife seemed to him to be a
perfectly faultless being. But he only said:

"Go and play me something, Emmeline. I
have n't heard the piano for so long."

And as the sweet familiar chords answered to the old magic of her touch, he got up and took the crocuses over to the piano, and set them down where she could see them, and she played on and on, nearly all the evening.

That was a very pleasant evening, and it taught them more than all their troubles had done. Things never came to such a very bad pass again. When, occasionally, this or that went wrong in the household, and the old Betty in Anson rebelled, Emmeline would strengthen her own resolution, and Anson's patience too, by crooning softly, as though to herself, a certain old nursery rhyme, beginning :

"Father's a nobleman, mother's a queen."

IV.

BEN'S WIFE.

BEN'S wife was a Hazeldean—a fact which that estimable woman rarely lost sight of. It was, perhaps, not to be expected that her husband and her husband's family should give quite due weight to the circumstance, but they were not allowed to forget it. At first, to be sure, the Pratts, who were themselves unpretentious sort of people, were not without some pride in the connection ; and even Old Lady Pratt herself did not object to letting fall the remark that "Ben's wife was a Hazeldean." An advantage like this, however, is one that should be sparingly used by its possessor ; and it must be confessed that Mrs. Ben was inclined to push it more than was quite well-judged, and that, as time went on, the Pratts allowed a suspicion of satire to creep into the statement which had been made at first in perfect good faith.

Yet there was much to be said in defence of Mrs. Ben. Perhaps no one who has not had the experience can justly estimate the sacrifice which the woman makes who relinquishes a name of three syllables, and one of such romantic and poetic associations as Hazeldean (if, indeed, there be such another) for a curt, unembellished monosyllable like Pratt. ·

Moreover, this foible, together with certain trifling vanities and affectations engendered by it, was almost the only flaw in an honest and kindly, if somewhat high-strung nature. " Ben's wife " was worthy of that title and proud of it too. She knew in her heart that she would rather have been Ben's wife than a duchess. Yet being securely Ben's wife for all time, and, as she devoutly believed, for all eternity, she still enjoyed the retrospective glory of having been a Hazeldean.

Her first son was unquestioningly named Benjamin ; but great was her rejoicing when the third child turned out to be a boy, and she could call him Hazeldean—Hazeldean Pratt ! She felt as though she had never appreciated her own name until this happy combination proved what a lustre it could throw upon a single commonplace syllable. The boy was called Hazeldean from his cradle, and no corruption of the name was ever tolerated in the family. The two elder children, when they first ventured to call their little brother "Hazie, for short," were promptly suppressed, and by the time the younger ones came to speech, the three syllables were so firmly established in their rights that they seemed one and indivisible.

Ben's wife was fond of dress, but Heaven forbid that that be accounted a flaw! She was a woman of excellent taste, thanks to which her house and her person were always as pleasant to look upon as the fashions of the day would permit. When the large hoops came into vogue, she was forced into them, as it were, for she would have been unpleasantly conspicuous without them. Yet she was never betrayed into extremes, and would have nothing to do with the "floating bell," when that climax of crinoline exaggeration appeared upon the scene.

In her house she was more independent still. It was a square house, modest, yet roomy, with the inevitable cupola on top. The house was painted gray with darker gray blinds, to suit the taste of the mistress, who disapproved the prevailing white and green of the suburb where she lived. When she refurnished her parlor, some fifteen years after her marriage, she boldly rejected the brilliant crimsons and liberal gildings of the period in favor of quiet colors. She chose a carpet of olive-brown Brussels with a dull red palm-leaf pattern, and window hangings of olive brown rep and plush, the effect being lightened by inner curtains of the finest and whitest muslin. Her furniture and her wall-paper were in soft neutral tints such as would to-day be called æsthetic, though they were little appreciated at that time, even by Ben himself. Indeed, if the truth were known, Ben, when he gave his wife *carte blanche* for refurnishing, had been dazzled by the most resplendent visions of red velvet sofas and a red velvet carpet bestrewn with baskets of pink and white roses, similar to, but even surpassing in brilliancy, the possessions of his wealthy brother-in-law James Spencer. His cheerful resignation when this glittering bubble of his fancy was pricked by the delicate point of his wife's finer perception, only showed what a thoroughly good Christian Ben was, and the amiability with which he submitted to the olive browns was eventually not without its reward. For many years after, the wheel of fashion having taken another turn, he had the satisfaction of seeing his neighbors revolutionize their houses at great expense, for the sake of bringing about the very condition of subdued harmony which had so long reigned under his own roof. Then it was that Mrs. Ben, who had meanwhile become an old woman, reaped a belated harvest of praise, and rejoiced in the consciousness of having proved herself to have been thirty years in advance of her time.

But this is a digression.

At the date in question, though the olive browns had not yet found their justification, Mrs. Ben, or Martha, as she was more familiarly called, had won a reputation as a very safe authority in matters of taste.

She was now the mother of five children, ranging in age from eighteen-year-old Ben down to little Eddie, a small mischief of five. She lavished upon them an adoring affection, yet she was not an over-indulgent mother, for she had very well-defined theories in regard to education. Her husband, secure in the conviction that his children would get all the training they needed without his doing violence to his own inclinations in the cause of discipline, was not afraid to spoil them to his heart's content ; and there was no denying that he, with his good-humored smile and sly jokes, had, all unconsciously, stolen many a march upon his wife in their young affections.

Ben had a great respect for his wife's theories, though he himself did not possess the sign of one. She, on her part, could forgive him the lack, since her own pet theories found an embodiment in his person. He was her ideal of what a man should be—an exemplification of all the broad virtues which she considered essential in a manly character. He had courage, integrity, good judgment, and equanimity. Moreover, his very failings were such as to endear him still more to his wife. In the first place he was forgetful, a shortcoming which tallied very satisfactorily with her theory that a man should be too much pre-occupied with great affairs to have a memory for small ones. Another source of gratification to her was his negligence in regard to his clothes and other belongings ; she having always entertained a lively contempt for a " finical " man. Best of all, he was open-handed to a fault, an admired weak-

ness which she joyfully corrected by the practice
of small and persistent economies, such as she
would have censured in him.

Martha's excitability of temperament, due, not
to nerves, but to an uncommonly active imagination, was a constant source of wonder to Ben,
though as years went by he had learned to treat
it lightly.

" Ben," she would exclaim at supper of a Saturday evening, while her eyes grew big with appre-
hension, and suppressed anxiety vibrated in her
voice—" O Ben ! Did you remember to order any
dinner for to-morrow ? " It was plain that the
vision of a starving family had suddenly terrified
her imagination.

Ben would take a spoonful of quince preserve
with the slow relish of an epicure, then look across
the table at his anxious helpmeet, with a deepen-
ing of the crow's feet which a life of quiet humor
had prematurely graven at the corners of his blue
eyes, and say, in a tone of inimitable self-complacency : " Yes, Martha, I got a little salt fish
and a cent's worth of asparagus."

Then the children would become hilarious over
their father's wit, Martha would draw a long sigh
of relief, untroubled by his jesting, and, behold,
the crisis was passed.

Ben's wife was a great reader of books, especially
of history ; and the histories of that day being
chiefly a succession of royal biographies, her
imagination was peopled with kings and queens.

She had always cherished a secret desire to behold a crowned head—a desire of which she was a little ashamed, in her republican heart, yet which rose to fever heat when the papers announced the coming visit of the young Prince of Wales to this country. His head, to be sure, had not yet been crowned, but was he not the next heir to the great throne of England, and was he not a youth in whom past and future united to produce an historic and romantic personage of the first water? And she, Martha Hazeldean (for so she still called herself in her moments of exaltation), she was to behold with her own eyes this royal boy. She eagerly read all the newspaper items which heralded and accompanied his visit to Canada, whilst *Harper's Weekly*, to which she was a subscriber, acquired a new and dramatic interest when portraits of the young prince began to appear among the illustrations of that admirable paper.

Ben was, of course, well aware of his wife's state of mind. If he had tried to do so, he could not have shared her feeling, and it never occurred to him to try. Ben was not sufficiently subtle to make any endeavors to cultivate sentiments which did not spring up of their own accord. He was republican to the core, and he could not see that Queen Victoria's son was necessarily more interesting than his own boys. That a great country, which had emancipated itself at the cost of blood and treasure from all the "folderol" of royalty, should be so ready to make a toy of it at the first opportunity, struck him as being quite as absurd as though his eighteen-year-old Ben were deliberately to go back to nursery rhymes and tin soldiers.

But though Ben did not share his wife's feelings he was as ready to gratify them as though they had been his own.

One pleasant afternoon in October, Mrs. Ben, adorned with a black silk apron and wearing a deep Shaker sun-bonnet, was out in the garden gathering a basketful of late nasturtiums, with which to put a touch of autumn sunshine into her olive-brown parlor. She had the faculty of disposing a bit of color just in the place where it was needed, and Ben had begun to perceive that these judicious touches gave their rooms a gayer, cheerier air, than all the downright crimson and gold seemed able to impart to the highly colored apartments which had once been his envy.

As she stooped to trace with careful fingers the windings of one of the delicate, brittle stems, she heard a step upon the gravel walk, and glancing up, beheld her husband coming toward her. His appearance so early in the day would have alarmed her had she not perceived a twinkle of roguish mystery in his eyes, which he was vainly trying to repress.

"Why, Ben !" she exclaimed, rising hastily to her feet and hurrying toward him. "What has brought you home so early ?"

" Is it early ? " he asked, innocently, making as though he would attack the citadel of the Shaker bonnet,

" Oh ! oh ! You 'll muss my hair ! " she cried, retreating.

" All done up for the afternoon ? "

" Of course it is," was the reproachful answer. " But, Ben, what has brought you home so early?"

" Old Pacer," he replied, this time with a still more quizzical look.

Ben was not the man to be hurried into an agreeable disclosure. He loved too well the pleasures of anticipation.

" Has anything happened ? " she asked, with growing impatience.

" Yes. I 've got home."

Ben was sometimes very trying.

" Come, Martha," he called, as she started, in simulated dudgeon, to walk away to her nasturtium beds, " let 's go and get some grapes."

" Good—ain't they ? " he observed, as they sat in the long arbor, eating the delicious Catawbas that grew in beautiful clusters just within their reach.

A pleasant silence fell upon them, broken only by the clucking of hens in a neighbor's yard, while the mellow October sunshine filtered through the thinning vines and checkered the backs of the two figures sitting amicably together. Martha had taken off her Shaker bonnet, and the sunshine slanted across the glossy black hair, which was brushed smoothly down over the ears, and passed in flat braids across the back of the head. She was not as much absorbed in epicurean delight as her husband seemed to be, but since he was in a teasing mood it was not worth while to talk to him.

Presently he spoke in an absent tone which seemed a trifle studied, while he held up a fresh bunch of grapes to his own admiring gaze.

"I don't s'pose, Martha, that you'd care anything about going to the Prince's ball?"

"The Prince's ball!" cried Martha, with a flush of excitement. Then, recovering herself: "Nonsense, Ben! What a tease you are!"

"Oh, then you wouldn't care to go? Well, I told Edward I didn't think you'd take any interest in it, and I felt pretty sure you wouldn't want the trouble of having a ball-dress made. I know I shouldn't."

"O Ben! Is there really going to be a ball for the Prince, and is Edward going?"

"Yes, Edward's going, and he thought maybe, as Lucia was in mourning, you might like to take her place and go with him. But I didn't s'pose you'd care much about it."

Martha's face glowed, and Ben's countenance was simply brimming with satisfaction as he watched the dawning upon her of this great, this stupendous idea.

"O Ben! you know I should like to go! Of course you said yes; now didn't you? Ah, don't tease! Come, tell me all about it."

Then Ben, having sipped his cup of pleasure long enough, proceeded to drink it down in generous draughts; for he loved, of all things, to make Martha's eyes shine.

For the next ten days Mrs. Ben was in a whirl of excitement. In the first place, there was the gown to be bought and made. She decided upon a "moiré antique," a silk then in the height of fashion, and which she considered economical, because of its great durability. She was divided in her mind between several neutral tints. One was called "ashes of roses"; another rejoiced in the euphonious name of "monkey's breath." When she finally fixed her choice upon a rich "mauve," Ben could not be persuaded to call it anything but "ashes of monkeys." But to Martha, nothing which concerned the ball seemed a fit subject for mirth. It was really a solemn occasion to her, this entering into the immediate, the actual presence of royalty. The only difficulty was that it engrossed her thoughts too much. She felt it; she regretted it; yet do what she would, she could not keep her thoughts fixed upon any other subject.

She had not dared entrust the making of so grand a gown to little Miss Plimpton, who went out by the day, and had hitherto contented the ambition of the family, and she had thus fallen a victim to a fashionable dressmaker, who had the reputation of disappointing her customers. Hence, in the days that were to elapse before her gown

should come home, poor Martha did not have a
moment's peace of mind. Questions also arose
of the very highest importance in regard to the
fashion of the dress, which she alone could
decide. Should the skirt be looped in five festoons, or six? Should the trimming be of black
lace, or white? Was llama lace sufficiently rich
for a Prince's ball, or did etiquette demand "real
thread"? On the one hand, llama lace was much
cheaper, but then it was quite inferior. And is
not the best the cheapest, when judged by true
standards? Thread lace, for instance, could be
handed down from generation to generation, and
would always be valuable. It was almost like
real-estate, or diamonds. If she only had diamonds to wear, by the way! But alas! though
she was a Hazeldean, her share of the family
jewels consisted in a pair of topaz ear-rings
and a set of turquoise; both of which were
manifestly unsuited to a state occasion. Even
the diamond ring which Ben had given her
on their tenth anniversary would be concealed by
her glove.

These, and like perplexities and speculations,
were chasing each other like mad through her
brain while she went about her household duties,
and, sad to say, even when she sat in church.
Strive as she might the next Sunday, she could
not rid her mind of the idea that the number of
festoons in her skirt was to be settled by the
number of heads in Mr. Hawley's sermon. And

when he wound up on "fifthly," so preoccupied
was she in trying to picture to herself the "effect"
of the five festoons thus decided upon, she
scarcely heard the salutary admonition, "Fix not
your hearts upon the things of this world."

None of the Pratt family had thought of such
a thing as going to the ball, and indeed it was
well that they had not. For boasting, as they
did, but few connections in high life, they might
not have gained admittance. Martha's brother
Edward, on the other hand, had married the
daughter of a "merchant prince," (a fitting
alliance for a Hazeldean), and he lived in the
city, where he was quite a personage. It was,
therefore, most natural that he should come to
the fore on occasions like the present.

The Pratts, however, though themselves too
stanch in their republicanism to regret their
own exclusion from the ball, were far from
indifferent to Martha's coming elevation. They
only half approved the expensive new dress,
indeed, on the ground that she was not
likely ever to have another chance to wear it,
but they were none the less eager to see her
in it, and there were few persons among their
large acquaintance who had not been informed
that " Ben's wife was going to the Prince's ball."
Whence it is fair to conclude that they were not
positively ashamed of the circumstance.

Old Lady Pratt alone held out against the
popular current of curiosity and excitement. She

had a vivid recollection of the War of 1812, and
of the burning of public buildings at Washington,
and to her the British were, and would always
remain, "the enemy." As to "Martha's craze,"
she contented herself with one bit of sarcasm,
which gave her much gratification and hurt
nobody. She told Harriet, her eldest daughter
and confidante, that she "s'posed Martha was
countin' on gettin' a chance to tell the Prince
that she was a Hazeldean."

For her own part, Old Lady Pratt was convinced that she would not have gone to the
window to look out if the procession had passed
through Green Street ; a degree of patriotism on
the old lady's part, which was, happily, not destined to be put to the test.

The ball was to take place on Thursday evening, and on Wednesday morning the Prince actually did arrive in Boston. The two boys, Ben
and Hazeldean, who went to school in town,
witnessed the august entry into the city, but
the rest of the family succeeded in curbing their
impatience until the grand procession which was
announced for the next day. Mrs. Ben awaited
the return of the boys with the keenest interest.
She was somewhat disappointed in their report,
in which the "Light Dragoons" and the crowd
of spectators played a more conspicuous part
than the Prince himself. To her urgent inquiries
in regard to his Royal Highness, these unsusceptible young republicans had nothing more

definite to say than that they "guessed he was well enough."

The grand gown had not yet arrived, but during supper a messenger, who had been sent to inquire about it, came back with the cheering assurance that it was coming in an hour. Thereupon the boys were despatched to tell Aunt Harriet and the girls that their mother would try on the dress as soon as it should arrive, and would be glad of their opinion. Little Eddie, who was somewhat hoarse, and was in wholesome fear of missing the procession next day, submitted to an early bed, but all the rest of the family sat awaiting, with bated breath, the arrival of the gown. It was a tedious evening, for the faithless dressmaker did not redeem her promise until nearly ten o'clock. In fact, Harriet and the girls were on the point of departing when the door-bell rang, sending a tidal wave of excitement over the stagnant waters of the company.

The gown was displayed with much ceremony, and all agreed that it was "both handsome and genteel." Harriet and the girls helped put it on, and so satisfying was the effect that the wished-for jewels were scarcely missed. Indeed, something of the translucent light and glow of gems seemed to emanate from the mother-of-pearl fan with which Edward had thoughtfully presented his sister, and which lent a peculiar air of distinction to the toilette.

Late as the hour was, they all lingered a long

MARTHA.

time, chattering and admiring and speculating as
to the impending glories. The boys, being sleepy
after the conflicting duties and excitements of
the day in the city, were the first to disappear.
Then the Pratt girls were sent to bed, and presently Ben escorted his sister and nieces home,
leaving Martha in solitary possession of her own
magnificence.

While the voices of her departing guests were
still audible on the stairs, Martha, who could no
longer restrain her impatience for a complete
view of herself, mounted upon a chair before her
toilet-glass. From this eminence she could see her
voluminous skirts to great advantage, and even
the open-worked stockings encased in bronze
slippers were visible. The head, to be sure, was
not included in the reflection—a fact which quite
escaped her notice ; for Martha's vanity was of a
singularly impersonal kind, and she was as unconscious of any charms of countenance as she
was of the graces of disposition which others
prized in her. It was the gown, and that alone,
which commanded her respect and admiration.
She stood there so lost in contemplation of its
beauties that she scarcely noticed that her guests
still lingered in the passage-way, till she heard
the heavy thud of the front door closing upon
them.

A sudden hush ensued. She stood upon the
chair, turning slowly round and round after the
manner of the lay figures in the shop-windows,

when suddenly she became aware of a strange, muffled sound. She paused, straining her ear to listen. What was it? Her heart stood still beneath the stiff breastplate of moiré antique. Could it be burglars? No; it was too early, and there were lights burning. Was it the wind? The wind never made a sound like that. And even while she tried to reason about it, the conviction seized her that it was a creature in distress. Only for a moment did she stand motionless, her eyes dilating with dread, the blood surging to her heart. Then, with a stifled cry, she sprang from the chair, flinging far from her the fan which she had held in her hand, and rushed to her dressing-room, through her dressing-room to little Eddie's chamber beyond; for—oh, terrible certainty!—it was from his room, from his bed, from his lips, that the blood-curdling sound came!

"My darling! my precious! what is it?" she cried, bending over him in mortal terror. "Speak my darling! speak, Eddie! Tell mother."

But the cruel gurgling and gasping were the only answer. With shaking hands she struck a light. There lay the poor little fellow battling for his life, his face purple, his eyes bright with distress.

She opened the entry door, and fairly flew to the boys' room. "Ben! Ben!" she cried, "run for the doctor! Eddie is dying of the croup! Run for your life! Hazeldean! go for Dr. Baxter; Dr.

Walton may be out. Run, boys! Fetch some one—any one! Run!"

The boys were on their feet in an instant. In another moment she was at the child's bedside, trying one ineffectual remedy after another. Her slender science was soon exhausted, all to no purpose. The struggle went on in a succession of alarming paroxysms. Then she sat upon the bed and held the suffocating child in her arms, trembling in a despairing knowledge that she could not help him, yet with the deep overwhelming urgency of a mother's love, which cannot credit its own impotency. She held him close, one of his little hands convulsively clasping hers, the small curly head pressed hard against her breast. Oh! the pathos of those baby curls, and that drawn, agonized baby face!

"In a minute, my precious!" she kept saying, "in a minute the doctor 'll come and make you well—just a minute, my poor darling. It 'll be over soon."

Over? *How?* As she spoke the words a desolating fear swept all her faith away, and suddenly, as in a flash of light, those other words, unheeded and forgotten, struck upon her memory: "Fix not your hearts upon the things of this world."

She looked down with a quick pang of remorse upon the stiff moiré antique. Alas! she who would have enfolded her darling in the softest textures, must see him lie in his extremity against

the cold, untender surface of this hateful gown!
The poignancy of that thought was almost more
than she could bear, and in the sudden rush of
remorse and terror all her innocent vanity stood
distorted into the guise of sin.

' "My God! my God!" she prayed, as she had
never prayed before, "I have been a wicked,
worldly woman! Oh, my God! have pity!"
No other words came, but all through those interminable minutes while she waited for help, "Have
pity!" she prayed,—"have pity!"

And suddenly, like an angel of deliverance,
the doctor stood before her. He stooped and lifted
the child from her arms, saying: "Don't be
frightened, Martha, we'll save him yet." And
she no more doubted his word than she would
have doubted him had he indeed been an angel
sent straight from heaven in answer to her prayer.

By two o'clock all was quiet and the child was
sleeping peacefully.

"Come, Martha," Ben said, putting his hand
on her shoulder as she sat by the bedside, still clad
in the moiré antique. "Come, do go to bed, the
doctor says there is nothing to fear, and I'll sit
up with Eddie. You won't be fit for the ball
to-morrow."

"The ball! the ball!" she repeated. "Oh,
Ben!"

But she went and changed the ball dress, shud-
dering as she listened to its stiff rattle, and then,
in a soft wrapper, she lay down upon the bed be-

side her boy. All night she listened to his easy, regular breathing, and all night long there was such a thanksgiving in her heart that she could not sleep.

The next day the child was quite himself again, trotting about the house, as active and as naughty as he had ever been in his life. He told his sisters he had had a "bad dream." It had, indeed, been a bad dream, a nightmare, which in his mother's eyes threw its ominous shadow upon all that had preceded and all that was to have followed it. No amount of reasoning could induce her to go to the ball, nor could she bring herself to look upon that terrible midnight hour as anything but a punishment and a warning.

"I can't help what you say, Ben," she protested with a fervor which he only half understood. "I've been a wicked, thoughtless woman. If I had n't had my heart 'fixed upon the things of this world,' I should n't have been parading about in that moiré antique dress, talking so fast that I could n't hear that precious child gasping for the breath of life. Think of it! only think of it! A little helpless child lying at death's door, while his mother's head was so full of princes and balls that she had forgotten she had a child to her name! No, Ben, I would n't go a single step. It would be tempting Providence. And besides," she added, giving what was, after all, the true reason, "I could n't."

"And Edward?" urged Ben, whose argumen-

tative powers were not great. "And Edward?
And that handsome gown?"

"Edward will have to go without me. And
the gown?" She paused an instant, while a
familiar look came into the ardent face. "Why,
the gown will make over nicely for one of the
girls when they are grown up. You know, Ben,
the colors I choose don't go out of fashion. The
Hazeldeans all have good taste."

Ben was consoled and relieved. Martha might
give up the ball—though he did n't see the sense
of it,—but she had not changed her nature yet ;
she was still a Hazeldean.

That day all the family but the inconsolable
Eddie and his mother went to town to Uncle
Edward's office, to see the procession escort the
Prince to the State-House. They came home with
glowing accounts of the fine display. Even Ben,
the heretic, had found it surprisingly interesting
to be looking straight down out of his own republican eyes at the future King of England, and he
owned as much.

"And to think, Martha, that you should n't
see the Prince after all !" he said at supper.

"Had n't you better change your mind, and go
to the ball?" he added, coaxingly ; for a moral
impossibility is a difficult thing to make other
people understand.

Martha was at that moment engaged in the
motherly office of drying the fingers of her youngest, who had been surreptitiously dabbling them

in his bowl of milk. She was thinking how she adored that little, chubby, mischievous paw, and "the things of this world," including the Prince and all his train, seemed to her very remote and indifferent.

"No, Ben," she said, "I don't care anything about the ball."

This was more conclusive than the ardor with which she had met his previous appeals, and Ben gave up the contest.

Perhaps the only person in the family who wholly sympathized with Mrs. Ben's feeling was her sharp little mother-in-law. When news was brought her of Martha's "foolish notion" of not going to the ball, just because Eddie had had the croup in the night—and not the real croup at that, her informant added,—Old Lady Pratt behaved in a very disappointing manner. In the first place, she took off her spectacles and rubbed them vigorously with her folded pocket-handkerchief before she spoke ; a thing she did, only when a good deal moved ; and then she said, with unusual warmth, "Martha 's a good woman, I declare for 't, if she *is* a Hazeldean !"

V.

A YANKEE QUIXOTE.

NOW, Jane Bennett, you ain't no call to fash yourself about William," said Old Lady . Pratt, looking over her steel-bowed spectacles at her daughter. "William 's got too good a head-piece to think jest as other folks do about every thing, and you might as well give up, fust as last, expectin' him to be cut and dried in his opinions."

Mrs. Henry Bennett, of Westville, who was paying her mother a visit, never let conversation languish for lack of a retort.

"I don't know 's William 's got any better right to his opinions than other folks have to theirs. And it 's my opinion that he 's disgracing the family with his wrong-headed talk."

Old Lady Pratt bridled. "Ef the family never gits no wuss disgraced than that, I guess there wont be no great cause for blushin'."

"Well, Mother!" snapped Jane. "You always did take William's part. I don't know 's we 'd ought to expect you to change in your old age!"

Old Lady Pratt was not fond of bickerings, so she let this thrust pass without rebuke.

Jane Bennett, as her mother had made a point of calling her, ever since she persisted in marrying contrary to the best advice, was something of a thorn in the old lady's flesh. One could see that, as often as the two women talked together. Jane was superficially almost the counterpart of her mother : in appearance, small, dark, and erect. But in her the decision of her mother's character took on the form of obstinacy ; the wholesome tartness of the elder woman's speech, had, in the younger, degenerated to acidity. Old Lady Pratt was distinguished by a certain liberal mindedness. With some few exceptions she was open to new ideas and tolerant of innovations. Jane, though very much given to harboring fixed ideas, was inclined, when once her mind was turned in a new direction, to go to extremes. When homœopathy, for instance, came into vogue, she not only accepted it for herself, but she pushed her son, ignorant and untrained, into a pretence of the practice of it. The wrong thus wrought he discovered, and set right as far as in him lay, but Jane Bennett never suspected the harm she had done. She had not a keen scent for her own mistakes, and her self-complacence was, therefore, rarely disturbed. As few people ever argued with her, she had not that familiarity with opposition which more yielding natures early acquire. Hence she found it impossible to reconcile herself to the quiet declaration of a heresy with which her brother William had recently startled her.

It was the troublous autumn of 1860. Abraham Lincoln's election had struck terror to the hearts of the conservative part of the community. Many a man who, four years later, was to regard that plain backwoodsman as the hero and savior of the nation, shrank from the impending consequences of his election. William Pratt was one of the conservatives.

"The South will secede," he had declared with conviction, when the election was discussed in family conclave.

"Then we 'll teach them a lesson !" said his sister Jane, vindictively.

"I suppose we shall," William admitted, "but we have n't any business to. They have as good a right to go out of the Union as they had to come into it."

For a moment even Jane was speechless. Then she said with withering sarcasm : "Perhaps you think there 's nothing wrong about slavery ?"

"You 've found me out, Jane. I will not deceive you. If the South should win, I propose to buy a cat-o'-nine-tails and a brace of bloodhounds, and apply for a place as overseer."

And that was all Jane could get out of her brother on the subject. His flippant jest about slavery could not be taken seriously, but at least it was clear that he believed in the right of secession, and she made the most of that.

Jane did not love her brother William. The two were "born to fight," as their placid, easy-going father—now at rest—had long ago declared. Jane's marriage and removal to another town might have brought about a truce, had she not carried with her the rankling memory of one of William's very worst and most reprehensible speeches. When all the family were up in arms about her predilection for Henry Bennett, William had said to his mother—and Jane had overheard the taunt: "We may as well make up our minds to Jane, Mother. There's no use in trying to reason with her, since she's got too old to be spanked."

It was certainly a most indecorous as well as disrespectful remark, and one which Jane had every reason to resent. How could she be expected, after that, to feel a proper gratitude, when the offender subsequently loaned her husband fifteen hundred dollars, without interest and with but small hope of return? What if this timely help did enable Henry Bennett to set up for himself in his trade of optician? What money obligations could atone to a really noble mind for a personal insult? Henceforth Jane nursed her grievance and hated her brother to her heart's content.

This was not the only time that William Pratt had "tied a knot with his tongue which he could not untie with his teeth." He was not a bad-tempered man himself, but he was often the occasion of bad temper in others. He had his enemies, men who, with or without reason, regarded him with strong antipathy, who hated the way he held his head and disliked the fashion of his canes. But he rarely put himself out for the sake of conciliating them. His own path had not been so smooth that he should feel the necessity of strewing rose-leaves under the feet of his fellow-creatures. There was, perhaps, more tenderness in his nature than he would have been willing to acknowledge, but it was not often called out now-a-days.

While yet a very young man, he had loved and married Isabel Allen, a woman peculiarly suited to him. There had been no disillusionment during the three happy years that followed —hardworking years, dearer to him than the hope of heaven. When a malignant disease robbed him, at one stroke, of his wife and boy, he felt that he had had his day, and he doggedly set himself to do his duty in an arid path. Though an unpopular man he soon earned the title of "public-spirited citizen." People learned that while an appeal to his feelings was not apt to be successful, an appeal to his reason, and to his sense of justice was rarely made in vain. It was the latter appeal that he yielded to when he thought he had discovered that Edna Brown had fallen in love with him. It happened about five years after the death of his wife. He did not particularly admire Edna Brown, though he was aware that most men did, and he would greatly have preferred to lead his own life, unhampered by new ties. But if Edna, who never concealed what she would have called her feelings, thought he could make her happy, he would not let his preferences stand in the way of her trying the experiment. Having married her, he was an excellent husband. Anything within reason that she wanted she might have. He was doing a good business in cotton, going to his office in the city every day, after the manner of suburbans —and in the course of time he built a very fine house, entirely in accordance with his wife's somewhat high-flying notions. Had Edna been exacting in the matter of sentiment he might not have found it so easy to content her, but as time went on it gradually dawned upon his plain, masculine intelligence, that perhaps, after all, Edna's infatuation had not been purely a tribute to his personal attractions. Such a discovery is not altogether pleasant to a man, even when the opposite state of things might be embarrassing. But William Pratt took it philosophically. He subjected his own physiognomy, mental and physical, to an impartial scrutiny, and he arrived at the conclusion that he had been a fool for his pains. That somewhat heavy countenance, with thick, bristling eyebrows and firm-set mouth, was not calculated to attract any woman, least of all an Edna Brown ; that caustic tongue that had estranged so many friends was hardly adapted to wooing. He must have changed a good deal, he reflected drearily, since last he looked into Isabel's eyes and read their adoration. Poor Edna! Perhaps after all he had cheated her out of what most women want. And from that time forth there was an added touch of kindness and solicitousness in his dealings with her, which filled Edna with satisfaction, as showing that she had kept her husband's affection longer than many women do.

There were three children, Mary, the eldest, being now fourteen. Their father was fond of them all in his undemonstrative way, though he loved them with an unconscious mental reservation. Once there was a discussion in his hearing on the subject of the English law of primogeniture. He took no part in the talk himself, but his mind reverted to the two-year-old boy he had lost so long ago, and it seemed to him that there was, after all, something peculiarly strong in the claims of one's first-born. His children, in their turn, found him a sufficiently kind and indulgent father, though they were not on terms of intimacy with him. At Christmas-time he took pains to find out their secret wishes. If the little girls sometimes incurred their mother's displeasure by tearing or soiling their clothes he was ready to intercede for them. If Willie, the baby, bumped his head and roared with pain and temper, it was his father who patiently sopped the bruise with cold water and told him not to cry. Yet William Pratt was not one of those fathers whose children cling about their legs and stand on the rounds of their chair, and the little ones thought nothing of going to bed without bidding him good-night.

With his nephews and nieces the case was not altogether different. They had a certain regard for him, largely induced by the transfer, from his pocket to theirs, of pennies, dimes, or quarters, the magnitude of the offering being carefully adapted to the age of the recipient. He liked to see them happy, and he did not know any other way of making them so. Yet there was not the same spontaneity in their affection for him, as in their love for Uncle Ben, whose small coins were not more migratory in their disposition than Uncle William's, but who had the gift of pinching their cheeks in a manner to rouse their deepest feelings, and who could tip them a wink worth more than money.

· William's best friend was his mother, but even she was not his confidante. She had been very proud of his conquest of Edna Brown, the belle of Dunbridge, and she took his happiness for granted. If Old Lady Pratt had a favorite child, that child was William. She delighted in his sharp sayings almost as much as in his successful career and his singular uprightness. In fact the latter sometimes cost her a pang, so frequently did it conflict with her son's own interests.

Only a day or two after Jane's visit William came in to see his mother after church, as was his custom. His deaf sister, Betsy, who was just a little afraid of William, had trotted off, nothing

7

loath, to help about the dinner. Old Lady Pratt having accomplished her devotions in a very thorough and satisfactory manner, had now put on her Sunday cap of white mull and her gold spectacles, and felt herself at liberty to consider worldly things.

"William," she said with much interest, "ain't cotton goin' up pretty fast?"

"Yes, there's been a big rise this month, and it's likely to go on if things don't quiet down at the South."

"Anson was tellin' me you'd got a large stock on hand. You'd oughter make a sight o' money."

"I don't expect to make more than usual."

"Why! I don't see how you can help it if you try."

"I sha'n't have to try so very hard. I shall sell my stock at a fair profit and no more."

"You don't mean to say that you'll sell below the market-price!"

"If the market-price isn't a fair one I don't propose to be governed by it."

Old Lady Pratt was quick but never hasty. She got up and pulled the shade down in one of the south windows, and then she put on a little knit shawl, a contradictory mode of procedure which showed that her mind was not on what she was doing. After that she resumed her straight-backed chair and gave utterance to her views.

"'Pears to me you're wrong, William," she said. "'T ain't as though you sold straight to the people. They ain't going to git the good of your generosity. You 'll only be a putting money into the pockets of the rich manufacturers. That 's plain enough to see.''

"If the manufacturers choose to pocket what does n't belong to them, that is n't my lookout. It 's hard times, and it 's going to be harder, and I don't mean to get rich on other people's misfortunes.''

This time Old Lady Pratt sat still and thought. Her silence was particularly impressive, as she had not even her week-day knitting to bridge it over. At last she said, reflectively : ''I 'm afraid you 're all wrong, William. 'T ain't the way folks do business—though I ain't sure that your father would n't have acted just so. And I declare for 't !'' with a sudden impulsiveness very unusual in her. ''Ef I was you, I believe I 'd *ruther* be wrong than right !''

And then to her son's unbounded surprise the self-contained old lady came over and gave him a hearty kiss—a thing which had not happened, except on state occasions, since he was a small boy.

William himself had no misgivings. He was accustomed to thinking things out for himself, and he had very little regard for '' consequences,'' that bugbear of many a thinker. It used to seem to him as though certain of the practical men of his acquaintance were always trying to hit the bull's-eye by aiming somewhere else. They fired away and reloaded, and fired away again, and collected their bag of game entirely regardless of the target, which, nevertheless, most of them had set up for themselves at the beginning of the match. He was quite ready to acknowledge that he missed his aim as often as not, but it was not for the sake of side issues. And as to this matter of the cotton, he did not care to go into the pros and cons of it. There was but one thing to be considered, and that was an innate repugnance to making money out of other people's misfortunes. He not only would not do it if it was wrong; he would have hated to do it if it had been ever so right.

On the question of the right of secession William Pratt had thought long and deeply, though perhaps a little confusedly. He lived in a very loyal community. The Union was something which most of his neighbors could not reason about. It was something sacred and unassailable as the moral law. If he tried to argue with them they looked at him askance, quite as though he had undertaken to defend kidnapping or burglary. It is possible that the opinion which he had arrived at was partly the result of a natural antagonism. William Pratt was so constituted that if he had been told every day of his life that a quadruped had necessarily four legs, it is more than likely that he would have come firmly to believe in the existence of a five-legged beast of that description.

He hated to be talked at, and was capable of loving his opinions as he loved his children, merely because they were his own. As the dreary anxious winter wore away, he did himself more than one ill turn by his rough handling of other people's prejudices.

One Friday evening in early April William went with his wife to prayer-meeting. He was a church member, but to Edna's chagrin he had never been able to overcome a certain reticence sufficiently to take an active part in such a meeting. It was an understood thing that he was not to be called upon, and being thus exempt he used regularly to attend on Friday evenings. It was one of the many things he did purely from a sense of duty.

The prayer-meetings of late had been particularly fervent. The community was in a state of unnatural excitement. The sense of an impending crisis brooded heavily upon all hearts, and in the strong tension of public feeling an appeal to divine aid was the natural impulse of every religious man. William had noticed with growing dissatisfaction the tendency of these meetings. The minister himself, who was a strong anti-slavery man, gave the tone to the proceedings. It seemed to William that a prayer-meeting should not be turned into an expression of partisan feeling. On this occasion he listened with ill-suppressed indignation to the prayers which followed each other in quick succession. Nearly

every one of them was an appeal for aid for the
Northern cause.   As he listened he was reminded
of the somewhat personal tone Jane's devotions
had once taken when he and she were children :
" Please God, make Mother box Willie's ears."

When, at last, one of the most eloquent of the
brethren openly called for the vengeance of the
Lord to be visited upon the offending South,
William felt that his turn had come.   To the
amazement of his wife, he rose deliberately to his
feet, and gave the premonitory cough customary
on such occasions.   The vestry-room was but
feebly lighted by kerosene lamps, one of which
was smoking badly.   In the dim, uncertain light
he could just see the furtive glances which were
turned towards him as the people in the sparsely
filled seats covered their faces with their hands.
When all heads were bowed, he began his prayer
in a voice a little harsh from contending emotions :
" God Almighty, we pray Thy mercy on our land.
We pray to be delivered from war.   We pray to
be delivered from disunion.   We pray, also, to
be delivered from the commission of injustice.
We pray Thee, O God, to deliver the North
from the calamities which we dread.   And we
pray Thee to deliver our sister, the South, from
the vengeance which we threaten.   Change
Thou the hearts of the North and of the South.
Deliver us from ourselves, that the terrors of war
and of disunion may be averted.   Forgive our
partisanship.   Forgive our evil passions.   Lead

us in the ways of equity and peace. Hear, O God, our prayer, not for our sakes, but for the sake of justice and humanity. Amen."

As the bowed heads were lifted at the close of this very unconventional prayer, none were turned toward the speaker. A constraint had fallen upon the meeting. Fortunately the time was up, and it was not necessary to prolong the session. The minister had risen to announce the closing hymn, when there was a sudden sound of cracking glass, and the broken chimney of the smoking lamp fell down on the heads and knees of the people below. There was a commotion in that corner until the flaring light was extinguished, and then the minister gave out the closing hymn: "Lord, dismiss us with Thy blessing." The inharmonious voices of the congregation rose and fell in lagging cadence upon the well-known tune, and then "the peace of God, which passeth understanding," was invoked upon the heads of the belligerent meeting, and William Pratt found himself at liberty to go out into the pure night air, beneath those clear burning lights of heaven, that neither smoke nor flare.

Edna followed him dejectedly. Why had she ever wished him to "take part"? She might have known he could not do it like other people. They walked on in silence for some distance, till at last she felt that forbearance was a weakness. Edna not infrequently found it her duty to remonstrate with her husband, though her reproofs were always couched in the most considerate language.

"I am almost sorry you made that prayer, dear," she began, gently. She usually called him "dear" when she was not pleased with him.

"Why?" he asked.

"Because I 'm afraid it gave offence."

"To whom?"

"Why, to all the people."

"It was addressed to the Almighty," he said curtly, and after that he said no more about it.

But as he met his fellow-Christians in the week that followed he noticed a marked coolness in their demeanor toward himself, and he rejoiced more and more that he had taken a stand.

Early in the following week his brother Ben looked in on him at his office—jovial, sweet-tempered Ben, who hated a row.

"How are you, Bill?" said he. "Got time for a smoke?" Ben was the only person who ever thought of calling him Bill.

They were soon established with their cigars, their feet on the office stove, Ben's chair tilted back at a genial angle. He presently came to the point.

"Look here, Bill. What put it into your head to stir up the meeting with a long pole last Friday evening? Anson is in a great state of mind. He says all the old Tabbies in town are by the ears about it."

" I don't know what you mean by a long pole,"
said William, gruffly ; " I asked the Lord to bless
the North and the South and to keep them from
laying hands on each other."

"Not much use in that," Ben declared.
"There 's bound to be a war."

"Think so? I 'm afraid you 're right."

For a time they puffed on in silence. Then
William asked :

"What shall you do about it if there is one ? "

"Do about it ? "

"Yes, do about it. Shall you fight ? "

"I? Fight? Good gracious no ! I 'm no
fighting man. I could n't stick a bayonet into a
sheep to save my soul."

"There 's a good deal that 's disagreeable
about war," William answered dryly. "I, for
one, would rather let the South go about their
business."

"We can't do that," said Ben, with conviction.
"We 've got the right on our side, and we 're
bound to maintain it."

" It all seems perfectly clear to you, apparently."

"Yes. I can't see that the thing 's got two
sides. But," brightening, "do you know, Bill,
it 's very lucky that you don't look at it as the
rest of us do, for if you did, it would be just like
you to go to the war yourself. You 'd be the
very fellow to go down there and get shot."

"It will certainly be just like a good many
poor fellows to do it. Fellows," William added

gloomily, "that have more to lose than some
of us."

"Nobody could have much more to lose than
you and I, Bill, with our wives and children."

William did not respond immediately, but then
he was not a particularly responsive man. At
last he said: "There's one thing you and I
would n't have to leave behind to keep our wives
and children company."

"What 's that?"

"Beggary."

Again there was a long pause.

"Well, Bill," said Ben, at last, as he finished
his cigar and turned to depart, "I think you 've
got hold of this thing by the wrong end, but your
heart 's all right, I 'll be bound!"

"Rubbish!" William growled. "Hearts
don't count. It 's heads we want and they 're
mighty scarce just now."

But all this was only the prelude. Men talked,
and argued, and discussed the war, and knew
very little of what they were talking about.
War is a grim word, but, after all, what is a word,
even the grimmest?

The terrible awakening which swept over the
land when the thunder of the first gun boomed
across the waters in Charleston Harbor was almost
as astounding, almost as appalling, as though
the name of war had not been spoken till that
day. It was on Saturday, the 13th of April, that
the echoes of that gun reached the North.

William Pratt, driving into town across the long bridge, saw hundreds of flags floating over the city. Their brave colors fluttering on the breeze seemed to speak of cheerful things, and for a moment the weight of anxiety and foreboding was lifted from his heart. But on the outskirts of the city he was undeceived. Newsboys were bawling the bad tidings at the top of their voices, men were standing in knots talking vociferously, and gesticulating in a manner unusual in an American crowd.

Pratt reined in his horse and bought a paper. He glanced at it, mechanically guiding his horse through the crowded streets. The headings were enough.

"WAR BEGUN!"

"THE SOUTH STRIKES THE FIRST BLOW!"

"FORT MOULTRIE OPENS FIRE ON FORT SUMTER AT FOUR O'CLOCK, FRIDAY MORNING."

He let the paper slip to his feet, and took a firm hold of the reins, to steady himself, not the horse.

The air seemed full of flying flags. Their bright colors fluttered through his thoughts in a strange, bewildering way. All the world was talking and gesticulating. He did not want to talk, he did not want to hear what was said. He knew enough. Too much. It was the worst. Nothing could mitigate that. He turned his horse's head away from the centre of the town, out toward the open country.

For three days William Pratt bore himself like a man indifferent to the great events that mastered every heart. He lived apparently unmoved by the tremendous emotions that surged about him. His face was set and hard. His eye was dull. His neighbors, when they saw him pass, murmured to one another the fatal word, "Secesh," fancying that they had the key to that stony indifference. And all the while his mind was in a tumult.

It was an inner vision rather than a thought that occupied him. The singular, irresistible power of a symbol had laid hold upon him. It was not the country he thought of, not the cause. It was the flag, the Stars and Stripes, that he had loved unconsciously for forty years, that riveted his mind. He saw them floating over Fort Sumter, brave and proud as they had floated over the city when he drove across the bridge on that Saturday morning. He saw them lowered at the bidding of a hostile gun.

For on Sunday news came of the surrender of the fort. The announcement was made from the pulpit. Strong men were shaken with sobs. Women's faces blanched. A little child in the pew in front of him pulled at his father's hand which hid his father's face, saying: "Don't ee cry, Papa." All day long that childish voice haunted William in meaningless reiteration. Yet he sat with tearless eyes and firm-set lips, seemingly shut out alike from the terror and the exaltation of the hour.

When the service was ended, and he stepped out into the sunshine, his wife and children stayed behind while he walked home alone.

On Tuesday William Pratt did a startlingly inconsistent thing. He deliberately enrolled his name among the defenders of that cause about which he had been so stubbornly sceptical.

When he came home from the recruiting office in the afternoon, he found his brother Ben sitting with his wife. It was just at dusk and the gas had not yet been lighted. William came in with a muttered greeting and took his seat in a large arm-chair where he leaned back heavily.

"Well, Ben," said he, "I 'm glad to find you here. I suppose you 'll be surprised to know that I 've enlisted."

"Enlisted !"

"Enlisted !"

Edna's voice was sharp and high, Ben's low with consternation. There was a dead silence before Ben spoke again with a somewhat unsteady accent.

"Why, Bill," he said, "I don't understand. I thought you did n't believe in the cause."

"You always sided with the South !" Edna urged, with feeble remonstrance.

" That was before they fired on the flag," her husband answered, in a tone of voice that she had never heard before.

Ben could not argue, but he plead, and Edna wept and lamented, and William sat there feeling as solitary in his newly awakened loyalty as he had found himself in the days of his heresy, till presently a slight figure in a bright plaid frock stole to his side, and a soft little hand was slipped within his own. It was his daughter Mary, who had sat by unobserved, and came to offer her mite of sympathy. He clasped the little hand tightly, and Mary sat on the arm of his chair all through the long discussion which followed.

At last Ben left them, and Edna went to dry her tears in her own room, and when they were alone together Mary said, in a very solemn voice: "Father, I wish I were a man so that I could go and fight for my country."

It had grown quite dark now. He put his arm about his little daughter and drew her down upon his knee, and then he said rather huskily: "Praise God that you are not a man, Mary. You might have to die for your country."

"I think that would be better than living," she answered, with the simple, straightforward conviction of a child.

There was a strange, new ache in William Pratt's heart, as he pressed the hot little cheek against his own. The flag no longer filled the whole horizon of his thoughts.

Happily for him, there was too much business to be got through in the short interval before he should join his regiment in camp, to leave much time for reflection or discussion. The final winding up of his affairs had to be in a great measure entrusted to his brother Ben, and it was at this time that Ben first learned that William had not taken advantage of the rise in cotton for his own enrichment. Ben was an honest man, but this was beyond him.

"Quixotic!" he growled. "Perfectly quixotic! Bill," he cried in desperation, "you need a guardian."

"Do I?" said William.

They were standing over the safe in his office, and as William looked down upon his brother a faint gleam of amusement came into his grave eyes. He was taller by half a head than Ben, and though the difference in their age was not great, he looked much the elder. With his stern, rugged countenance and strong frame, he presented a marked contrast to his blue-eyed, good-humored junior, whose short figure was getting stout but would never be powerful.

"Do I?" he asked again.

"Yes, Bill! you do! First you throw away your luck and then you do your best to throw away your life. I 'm blessed if I can see what right you have to cut into us all in this way, especially for a cause you never stood up for before."

"Queer that I can't make you understand," said William, with a contraction of the brows, as though he were trying to think out some elaborate explanation of a very simple problem. "I suppose you can imagine the case of mother, for instance, getting into a difference of opinion with a neighbor, and your admitting that he was as much in the right as she. But if he were to lift his hand against her, I reckon you would n't think twice before you knocked him down."

The trouble in Ben's face deepened. The allusion to his mother only made things worse. The old lady had "plenty of grit," but her eyes were so much brighter than usual when he called to see her that morning that he had felt anxious. She was an old woman and ought not to be called upon for the exercise of heroism.

William himself was too preoccupied to be very much alive to other people's feelings. Among all the confused experiences of that time of preparation and departure there was only one moment that stood out clearly in his mind, that dwelt with him in the weeks that followed, when he lay awake under the stars in the home camp, and later when he came into close quarters with the realities of war.

The apologetic embarrassment of his discomfited accusers made very little impression upon him, while even as to his wife herself, he seemed to have forgotten just what she did and said at the last. He could recall hardly anything about his parting with his brothers and sisters. He remembered the grip of the dry and wrinkled hand of age, when he kissed his mother, and that her brave old lips trembled slightly as they touched his. But whether she had said the word good-bye or had failed to say it he did not know.

In his breast pocket was a neat little pen-wiper, the covering worked in red, white, and blue worsteds in the shape of a flag, and in yellow silk were done "all the stars for all the States," little Mary had said when she gave it to him. "And you must use it, Father, when you write to us, and when you bring it home again it will have come true, and all the States will be in the Union, just as they used to be."

He had taken the child's face between his two large hands, and looked down with infinite wist-fulness into the clear young eyes.

"Mary," he had said, "I wish you and I had known each other a little better."

"Never mind, Father," the girlish treble sounded sweet and true as a bell. "When we meet again we shall be great friends."

Then he had kissed her forehead and held her very close, and she had stroked the front of his coat, the Union coat that he was to do his fighting in, until her mother came and claimed her right to weep upon his shoulder.

He thought of his clear-eyed, high-hearted little daughter, as he sat among the men of his company on the eve of the first great disaster of Bull Run and again as he went into action the next day.

The bullet that pierced his heart passed first through the little worsted flag, but it left the field

9

of stars unbroken. And the little flag was buried with him in Southern soil, a mute and hidden witness to the better time to come.

When that good time had come, when the humble testimony of those tiny golden stars had been fulfilled, the little Mary had grown to be a tall young woman, rather mature and thoughtful for her years. Many girlish fancies had passed away, many hard realities had come to take their place. But no ungentle years could rob her of her best heritage, her father's memory, nor did she ever lose faith in her parting words to him : "When we meet again we shall be great friends."

WILLIAM.

VI

A NEW ENGLAND QUACK.

"AND how 's Anson gittin' along?" asked Miss Grig, the proprietor of the thread-and-needle store next door, as she payed for the new glass in her spectacles. "I 've hear'n tell 's how he was makin' quite a success of his doctorin'."

Mr. Bennett's face dropped its business expression and took on a genial look of complacence.

"Oh, Anson! He 's doin' a great business. He 's cuttin' out the allopaths right an' left. Reglars, they call themselves, and my wife says that 's all right, for most on 'em 's reglar old Betties! Why, Anson 's got the best part of the practice in that country for miles round!"

"Well! It doos beat all, I must say, that a young man brought up to the spectacle trade should suddenly perk up and know so much 'bout folks' insides. I s'pose now, homepathic means home-made or somethin' of the kind."

"Like 's not," replied the proud father. "I always said the doctors round here might learn a thing or two of Mis' Bennett. She comes of an

131

oncommon smart family, the Pratts of Dunbridge, and she was about the smartest of the lot. It 's been a real eddication to Anson to be the son of such a woman."

Then the worthy man grew more expansive, and leaning over the counter with a confidential air he added: "Do you know, Miss Grig—(I don't want to brag, but this is betwixt you and me)—that boy 's used up one *hoss* a'ready !"

A look of horror came into the excitable countenance of Miss Grig. She gazed into Mr. Bennett's face through her neatly repaired glasses and gasped:

"What! For *pills !*"

While Mr. Bennett was explaining to his old friend, that the "hoss" had been used up by too much travel on the long country roads, young Bennett was driving the first victim's successor, at an easy pace along the East Burnham turnpike.

It was one of those soft days in early May, when the apple-blossoms are in their glory, and the balmy air quickens the heart with gladness. Anson Bennett's heart was beating to the tune of hope and joy. He felt to his finger-tips, the delicious spring awakening, and pleasant thoughts sprang up in his mind, as naturally as early buttercups from the sod.

Now this young man, with his well-favored, not unintelligent face, and an air of candor and good-will which went far to win the country people's confidence, was nothing more nor less than an impostor. Yet impostor that he was, he was first of all his own dupe. Homœopathy had but lately come into vogue, and the apparent simplicity of its principles had made it, or an unworthy travesty of it, instantly popular. Especially among New England housewives, who like to feel themselves equal to every emergency, the little wooden cases of bottles filled with palatable remedies for every ill, were welcome possessions.

"Why," Anson's mother had said, "it's just like the way Luther gave the Bible to the people! Think how long the priests had kept the religious doctorin' all to themselves."

The good woman had an ill-defined notion that doctrine and doctorin' had more similarity than that of mere sound. "I tell you, it's jest the same with the doctors. It's nothing but self-glorification that's always made 'em so secret about their learnin'. The Lord sets 'em a better example than that. The Lord promises to help folks that help themselves. But you'd think, to hear the allopaths talk, that a woman was committing some awful crime, when she gave a little nux vomica to a child that's got the snuffles, instead of running up a doctor's bill and being made to torture the poor little thing with nasty-tasting drugs."

Jane Bennett was, as her simple-minded husband took pride in remembering, a Pratt of Dunbridge, and she had inherited something of the "faculty," which has always distinguished that highly respectable family.

Marrying at a very early age—in opposition, let it be whispered in confidence, to her mother's wishes—and removing to the small manufacturing town where her husband pursued his calling, Jane Pratt had taken a step downward in the social scale. The ignorance which is the prerogative of sweet seventeen, had not been modified by contact with her betters, or even with her equals, and her self-confidence—sometimes called pigheadedness—had received no check. Hence she never suspected the undeniable fact that she was as ignorant of the true science of homœopathy as she was of the higher mathematics. And in spite of ignorance and pigheadedness, Jane Bennett was very successful with her nux vomica and belladonna and what not, and she had little difficulty in persuading her son of the soundness of her views. Anson had received much practical benefit from his mother's treatment of the small ills which had assailed him from time to time ; her methods seemed to him rational, her arguments just. When she finally gave him a little manual of "symptoms," and told him it would teach him homœopathy, there appeared, to his mind to be a great light thrown upon a hitherto dark and tortuous province of human experience. He was very young, very ignorant and very ambitious, and he was but too ready to believe that those little sugar-coated pills were the last and most comprehensive outcome of medical science, and that he, with the aid of his manual, and a fair stock of natural "gumption," was as well fitted as another to administer them judiciously. Eight months' practice on whooping-cough and measles, in a healthy country neighborhood, had only confirmed him in his self-confidence, and he had almost come to feel as though it were his own diagnosis (a word, by the way, which he valued highly) which fixed the nature of the disease to be treated.

He was now on his way to a patient—a mechanic living on the outskirts of the neighboring town of East Burnham—whose case he had pronounced to be a severe catarrhal cold, and had for some days past been treating accordingly. His heart swelled within him as he thought of his past success and future prospects, and all his meditations were tinged with the spring sunshine.

"What a heavenly-minded day this is," he said to himself; "and how pleasant it is to be driving along through this pretty country ! To think that I might have spent all my days behind Father's counter, waiting on fussy old ladies, if I had n't turned doctor ! "

His thoughts made a pause, while a picture rose before his mental vision.

" I wonder if Alice would n't like to be sitting side o' me, and driving along among the apple-blossoms ! "

The young man glanced wistfully at the empty seat beside him, and then at the blossoming trees on either hand.

"She 'd go well with the apple - blossoms. There 's so much pink and white about her, and she 's so sweet."

Then he fell into a wordless reverie, while his horse ambled lazily on. The dreamy stretches of pasture land, the soft spring air, and the fragrant apple-blossoms were all blended in his happy mood ; but the keynote of this delicate harmony was the pretty girlish face he looked upon with the "inward eye,"—pink and white and very sweet, but with a grace his fancy added, the grace of shy responsiveness. For the sweet face had not yet softened for him ; the clear eyes had not yet met his with answering affection. It was only that on such a day as this everything seemed possible to his young ambition.

" She 's proud, and she has a good right to be," he admitted to himself. " 'T is n't only that her father 's so well off and has been in the legislature. She 'd be just the same if her folks were nobodies. A girl like her," he told himself to-day for the hundredth time, " could n't be expected to marry a man of no account. It stands to reason she 'd look high. But a doctor with such a practice as mine, is a different matter."

An attractive smile lit up his face. " I know I could make her happy. There is n't anything I would n't do for her. She should have as nice

a house as any lady hereabouts, and lots of
flowers in her garden. I s'pose she likes flowers. Seems as though a girl like her must feel
sort of at home among them. I guess I 'll
send her a bunch next time I go home." He
looked again at the apple-trees, whose blossoming branches hung over the stone wall on either
side of the road.

"I'd like to send her a lot of apple-blossoms
now," he thought, "but I s'pose that would n't
be much of a compliment; they 're so plenty.
They do look just like her though."

A stray petal floated through the still air and
dropped upon his knee. He picked it up and
regarded it thoughtfully.

"Pity so many of them come to nothing,"
he mused. "I wonder why things should be
wasted so."

He often thought of the fragile waif, in after
years, when he remembered that day of blossoming of all sweet things in his own thoughts.

Dr. Bennett stopped his horse before a bare-
looking house, dropped the weight on the ground
with a professional air, and taking his medicine
case from the chaise, walked up the path. It
was with difficulty that he pulled himself together, and got himself back to real life. On
the threshold he paused a moment and looked
lingeringly upon the pleasant landscape, as
though some subtle premonition had told him
that he was turning his back for ever upon a

sweet spring world. Then he lifted the latch and entered into the chill shadow of sordid cares.

A woman met him in the little dark entry-way. She was a young, timid-looking creature, and little children were clinging to her skirts. Her cheeks were flushed and her eyes unnaturally bright. Anson thought he had never before noticed how pretty she was, and, stooping to pat the cheek of one of the children, he said, cheerily :

" Well, Mrs. Ellery, I hope your husband is doing well to-day."

" O Doctor ! " she answered, in a voice that sounded strained and weak, " I was just going to send after you. He 's been that bad all day, that I was afraid to wait till you 'd come."

A queer shock went through Anson, as he drew himself up and looked again into her face ; but he recovered himself instantly, and saying, " I 'm sorry you 've been anxious, but I guess we shall have him all right again pretty soon," he passed into the sick-room with her. The children remained huddled together in the dark entry.

The sick-room was on the north side of the house, and seemed chilly and comfortless. The patient lay with closed eyes on the bed. A strange, bluish pallor overspread his face, and he was breathing hard and painfully. Dr. Bennett took in his the hand that lay upon the calico counterpane. It was cold and clammy, and again that strange shock went through him.

At his touch the patient opened his eyes feebly, and looked up at him. But he closed them again, muttering something which the doctor failed to catch.

"I guess he's asking for Dr. Morse," said the wife, whose cheeks were pale again. "He's been asking for him all day, and I did n't know what I'd ought to do about it."

Dr. Morse, as Anson knew, was the family physician whom he had superseded. For a moment the young doctor's face looked hard and almost cruel. He had seated himself in the chair placed for him at the bedside, and was apparently absorbed in counting his patient's pulse. It was but a faint fluttering of life beneath his finger, and he felt a sinking at the heart as he tried to put his mind upon the count. He had never lost but one patient, as he often reflected with pride, and that was an aged man. Suppose James Ellery should die. Was it his fault? People must die, in spite of the doctors. It was only that this was almost his first fatal case, that it should take such hold of him. Yet, all the same, it was a sickening feeling to have a life which you were trying to hold slip from your grasp in this way.

His touch upon the wrist must have tightened, for the patient moved uneasily, and tried to draw his hand away. Dr. Bennett looked at his watch. Nearly five minutes had passed, and yet he had not counted the feeble pulse. He released the hand suddenly and turned to the woman standing beside him.

"Do you want Dr. Morse?" he asked.

"If you would n't mind," she said, hesitatingly. "I think it would comfort James. He 's been fretting about it all day."

"I will go for him."

"Oh, no! Don't leave *him*," she begged, with a frightened look towards the sick man. "I 'll send Willie Anderson next door," and she hurried from the room.

"I suppose that 's always the way," thought Anson, ratherly bitterly, yet trying to reassure himself by the reflection. "They lay every thing to the doctor, and I suppose now they 're sorry they ever left that old fogy, with his nasty drugs and his bloodlettings, and all his antiquated notions. But he looked from time to time uneasily at his patient.

It was a miserable situation, and every moment increased Anson's perplexity and distress. He got up and paced the room—for Mrs. Ellery did not return—and tried to cast off the terrible weight of anxiety. Then he paused and looked again at the sufferer. It was no wonder that his heart was lead within him. He was standing face to face with death—not death as he had seen it, coming to release a pilgrim bowed down with years and infirmity, but death, summoning the soul of a man in the prime and vigor of life. He seemed to see the grim spectre defying him, and he, who should have been armed to the teeth, stood weaponless, helpless as a child. A shuffling sound at the door startled him, and then he heard a childish voice whimpering—"Muvver! Muvver! Let me in!"

He went and opened the door and said sternly : "Your mother is n't here. Go away!" and the little figure turned and fled from the strange man, in whose set face the child had not recognized the doctor.

And still the mother did not return. She must have gone herself for Dr. Morse. Anson paced the room in growing anguish of spirit. It seemed like a horrible nightmare, and he flung his head back violently to wake himself. Yet he knew, with an insistent, grinding knowledge, that it was a nightmare from which there would be no awakening.

In after years when he looked back upon that day, one consolation remained to him in his shame and self-abasement. He had not carried on the pitiful farce a moment after it was revealed to him in its true light. Though his mind was not prompt to accept the bitter truth of his incompetency, a deeper consciousness of it was so borne in upon him, that he offered no remedy— gave no advice. From the moment when his finger touched the vanishing pulse, he ceased to act his miserable part. His feeble pleas for himself, his fretful accusations of others, were but surface disturbances.

As he sat beside his patient in the gathering twilight, listening to his labored breathing and feeble moanings, he looked upon the dying man with a passion of envy stronger, even, than his remorse. To die! To die! To escape from a life, maimed, ruined, as his own must be, if this were indeed no nightmare, but an inexorable fate.

There was a sudden sound of steps in the passage-way, and the door opened softly. A light streamed in from the lamp which Mrs. Ellery held in her hand, and at first Anson saw only her frightened face. But there, in the shadow, was the short, sturdy figure of Dr. Morse, the despised rival of the successful young practitioner. While Mrs. Ellery explained, in a hurried whisper, that she had not found Willie Anderson, and had herself been searching through the town for Dr. Morse, the latter stepped to the bedside, and made a hasty examination of the patient. He shook his head and Anson fancied that he heard the words—"Too late."

A baby's wail from the kitchen broke rudely upon the solemn hush, a door was opened, and the sound of fretful voices approached. Dr. Bennett stood an instant irresolute. Then he said, in a dry, hard voice : " I will go and quiet the children."

" Oh, if you would ! " said Mrs. Ellery, gratefully ; and Anson left the room, accepting it as his dismissal.

He went into the kitchen and humbly did his best to pacify the peevish, hungry little people who were quarrelling in the dark. He lit a lamp and got them some gingerbread from a high shelf in the cupboard, and presently they were standing around his chair, five little eager listeners, while he told them the story of Jack the Giant Killer. Curiously enough, he became so absorbed in the old tale, that he succeeded in detaching his mind, for the moment, from all that was real and painful, and, finding an unspeakable relief in this momentary oblivion, he continued his storytelling, relating, with a feverish earnestness and rapidity, the adventures of one after another of the nursery heroes.

An hour or more had passed thus, when suddenly a heavy step just outside the door smote upon his consciousness like a blow, and he stood up to meet his accuser.

Dr. Morse opened the door, and said, in a voice that sounded very much like a command : "I should be glad to have a talk with you, Dr. Bennett. Suppose we step out-of-doors.'

Bennett pushed the children rather roughly aside, and followed his summons. The stars were out, and the evening air was sweet with the fragrance of apple-blossoms. As he stepped off the low, flat door stone, Anson felt a sudden giddiness, and faltered in his gait. But the voice of Dr. Morse steadied him.

"Your patient is dead," he said, harshly.

"There's a neighbor woman in there with Mrs. Ellery."

They walked down the little path and back again.

"I thought I should like to know what your treatment of pneumonia is."

"Pneumonia!" exclaimed Anson, involuntarily.

"Yes, pneumonia. I assume that you concealed the nature of the disease out of consideration for Mrs. Ellery. You did not, of course, blunder in the diagnosis of so plain a case."

Anson made no reply.

"How long has your patient been ill?"

There was a sarcastic emphasis on the words "your patient" as often as the doctor spoke them.

"I was first called last Monday."

"H'm! Did he seem pretty sick then?"

"No. He only seemed to have a violent cold. He was feverish and coughed a good deal, and he complained of a pain in his side. But that went off after three days."

"How was his pulse?"

"Rapid, but pretty strong."

"And his respiration?"

"He seemed to breathe easily."

The elder man's lip curled scornfully. They were still pacing up and down the path to the front door.

"Let us step outside the gate," said Anson, "where we sha'n't have to turn so often."

As they opened the gate, Anson's horse turned his head toward his master and whinnied softly. It was singularly comforting. The horse, at least, believed in him, and looked to him for release.

" I suppose you know that the respiration must be closely watched. It 's a pity you can't speak more positively about it."

A feeling of irritation came over Anson. He resented being catechised, and resentment was a relief.

" I don't know what you could do about it now," he said, " if I chose to tell you."

" Oh ! then you kept yourself informed. That is well. What stimulant did you give him ? "

Here Anson seemed to feel the ground under his feet once more, and he said with decision : " Our school does not believe in stimulants."

" And nourishment ? " asked the doctor.

" He was too feverish to be given much nourishment."

" Too feverish for nourishment, and his pulse sinking to nothing ! Good heavens, man, you don't know what you are talking about ! "

Again there was a feeble flutter of self-assertion in Anson's harassed mind, and he answered, with a last attempt at dignity :

" You must remember, Dr. Morse, that you and I belong to different schools of medicine."

Here the doctor's patience gave out, and his wrath broke loose—

" Different schools ! " he cried. " Different schools ! You 're talking arrant bosh ! *Your sort* don't belong to any school under heaven. The Lord knows there 's no love lost betwixt me and the homœopaths. They 're a wrong-headed lot, and I should like to see the whole wretched fallacy uprooted and cast to the winds. But there *are* scientific men among them, who are neither knaves nor fools, and I won't have any body of scientific men insulted. Such men as you are the curse of any school—it is such men as you who have brought it into disrepute—it is such men as you——"

" For God's sake, stop ! "

The doctor turned, suddenly ashamed of his torrent of words, and looked at Anson, who had stopped in his walk, and stood clutching a thin rail fence, which creaked and wavered in his grasp. In the dim starlight his face looked drawn and deathly white.

" Do you feel ill ? " asked the doctor.

" Yes, mortally ill," said Anson, with a harsh laugh. " If you had a pistol about you, I think I could cure my own case quicker than you could."

" Here, take my arm—I 'm afraid I was a brute."

" We 're all brutes together," said Anson. " I don't want your arm. It is n't my body that you 've butchered," and he walked toward his chaise and began fumbling with the hitching rein. The doctor watched him uneasily, but did not venture to help him. When he had unfastened the rein, Anson lifted the weight a few inches, but dropped it again, and left it lying on the ground. As he got into the chaise he reeled slightly, and the doctor took a step forward. But he recovered himself without help, and when he was seated, he gathered up the reins and drove rapidly away. Dr. Morse stood looking after the black chaise top, as it disappeared in the darkness, and listening to the sound of the receding wheels.

"Who could have supposed that a quack had a conscience," he muttered, as he turned on his heel and walked back to the desolate little house.

Anson Bennett had gone down into a blackness of darkness infinitely more terrible than anything the good doctor conceived of.

One pleasant evening four days later, Dr. Morse sat in his office enjoying an hour of hard-earned leisure. The office was a plain, uninviting room, with oil-cloth on the floor, shabby old furniture, and an unsightly hole under the mantlepiece, where a stove-pipe did duty in winter time. But the doctor loved the place, and was never so comfortable as when sitting, as now, in his revolving-chair, surrounded by his well-worn books and dusty bottles, smoking the second half of a cigar. He smoked very slowly, waiting, after each whiff, to watch the blue incense curl and wind in a vanishing spiral.

To-night he was taking his pleasure more slowly and thoughtfully, if possible, than was his wont. In fact, he once let his cigar go out entirely, a thing which he prided himself upon just avoiding, in his skilful prolongation of the indulgence. He was ruminating upon Mrs. Ellery and her perplexities, which occupied his mind as often as it was free from immediate demands. Between whiles he permitted himself an occasional fling of scorn at that "miserable young quack." When the cigar had been long enough extinguished for the smoke to have yielded to the perfume of the blossoms which floated in at the open window, the delicate odor recalled so vividly the circumstances of his talk with Bennett, that he felt a return of that compunction and soft-heartedness which he had come to regret, and he hastily struck a match and relighted his cigar.

Presently there was a step on the gravel walk, and, looking up, the doctor saw the object of his indignation approach his door. As the young man entered, Dr. Morse rose with conflicting feelings. He did not immediately offer his hand, and when he did so Bennett had seen his hesitation and withheld his own.

"You need n't mind about shaking hands," he said, with a touch of dignity which seemed scarcely compatible with the situation as the doctor looked at it. "I have n't come to you on my own account, and I won't trouble you for long."

The two men sat down and were silent for a moment. The cigar had again gone out, and the scent of the blossoms filled the room. The voices of the doctor's wife and daughters came in at the open window, and made upon Bennett an indescribable impression of home and comfort. This was what he had looked forward to. Honor and love and a happy home. And the short-lived blossoms whose sweetness had mingled with his dream, had not yet passed away! But the doctor was waiting for him to speak.

" Dr. Morse," he began, " you will not be surprised to hear that I have given up doctoring, and you will, of course, understand that the only wish which I can have, or at least which I have any right to have, is to make what reparation I can to the family of my unhappy patient."

The doctor was not only surprised, but fairly taken aback by this speech. He repeated the young man's word mechanically.

" Reparation. Yes, of course, of course. Quite natural."

But his mind was undergoing another awkward change of attitude toward quacks.

" You would have heard from me before this," Bennett continued, " but I thought it best not to trouble you until the matter was settled. I have been home and talked things over with my poor father. It comes hard on him, but he looks at it as I do, and he will take me back into business."

" What 's your business? " asked the doctor.

" We are opticians."

" H'm ! Do you like the trade ? "

" I don't know what that has to do with the question. We 're in it, and it gives us a fair living. What I have come to ask about is Mrs. Ellery. I shall, of course, consider myself responsible for the support of the family, and I want you to act for me in the matter. I have inquired about her husband's earnings, and I think I can spare very nearly that income from the beginning. Your part would be to invent some reason for her receiving it without betraying me. I 'm afraid she would n't take the money if she knew all. Do you think you could arrange this ? "

" Easily enough," said the doctor. He examined his small fraction of a cigar with much apparent interest, and then he added : " I suppose Mrs. Ellery has a mind, but I have never known her to use it. She would believe that the ravens were feeding her if I told her so."

Anson was about to make some reply when the doctor asked, abruptly : " How long do you propose to keep it up ? "

" How long ? Always, I suppose."

" And when you are married and have a family of your own to provide for ? "

" I, married ? I shall never marry."

" Oh ! You can't be so sure of that at your age."

" I tell you I shall never marry."

" Have you never wished to ? "

Anson sprang impatiently from his seat and strode to the window.

" I wish you 'd quit your probing, Dr. Morse. I did n't come to talk about myself."

Dr. Morse rose, more deliberately, and followed him to the window, where the light was still clear. Bennett's face was under better control than his voice, but there was a change in it which the doctor recognized as permanent. A great wave of respect and compassion went through him.

" Young man," he said, in an altered voice, " I should feel it an honor if you would shake hands with me."

Flushing like a boy, Anson turned and looked into the homely face. The two men clasped one another's hands.

The next day Anson sat once more in his father's shop, plying with skilled fingers the handiwork to which he had been trained. Preoccupied as he was with bitter reflections, he was yet not wholly without consolation. His father's welcome was something. Mr. Bennett, garrulous in time of triumph, had few words on this occasion. When they entered the shop together on that first morning, he only said : " It seems real good to have you back, Anson. I 've missed you considerable," but Anson felt the grip of the kind hand all day long, and often, in the days to come, he seemed to feel again that friendly pressure. In the practice, too, of his trade was unlooked-for solace. The sense of mastery was peculiarly soothing to his wounded self-esteem, and it was then that he realized for the first time the satisfaction of being an expert. Had it not been for the frequent calls to the counter he might almost have lost himself in his occupation.

For the first few days after his return it was surprising how fast the Bennett custom increased. One after another of the neighbors came in with spectacles in need of repair, until Anson suspected them of ransacking their garrets in search of discarded glasses, merely for the sake of having a talk over the counter.

Among the first to appear was Miss Grig, with a pair of " specs ". belonging to her mother, which seemed " kind o' loose in the jints." Would Anson " jest see 'f he could n't tighten 'em up a bit ? "

Anson had begun to feel the grim humor of the thing, and he made a pretence of tinkering the glasses a little before returning them.

" Thank 'ee," said Miss Grig, as she took them. " How much will that be ? "

" Nothing at all, Miss Grig. It is n't worth mentioning."

" Very much obliged, I am sure," said the old lady, evidently relieved. She had rather begrudged the price of her curiosity.

" We 're all so glad to see you back, Anson,"

she went on, with a comical accession of interest. "It seems so nat'ral to see you standin' there behind the counter. Only it 'pears to me you ain't lookin' quite so hearty as you was. Maybe you found doctorin' did n't agree with you. 'T was too confinin', 'praps.''

Miss Grig looked at him with her head a little on one side, like a bright-eyed, inquisitive cock-sparrow.

"No, it was n't exactly that," Anson replied, with an assumption of indifference. "The fact is, Miss Grig, I had come to the conclusion that I did n't know enough for doctoring."

"Now do tell. And we all heard you was so successful and hed sech a great practice. Why, your Pa told me——"

"Yes, yes! I know! Father was all right about that. I had plenty of patients. But I found it was a bigger subject than I thought for, and I was afraid I might be making mistakes and doing mischief if anything unusual turned up."

"An' I s'pose that idee was wearin' on you. Well, I don't know 's I wonder. The allopaths, now, do have a sight o' larnin'. My second cousin on my mother's side is bringin' up her son for a doctor, and there don't seem to be no end to the trouble and expense. But I s'posed 't was different with the homepaths. Them little pills seem so easy given and so easy took. An' if they don't do no good, I don't see 's they can

do much harm any way.   You did n't happen to
ketch yourself givin' the wrong kind now, did
you ? "

At this juncture another customer came in and
the small inquisition ceased, only to recommence
in another form.   Happily not many of his exam-
iners were as searching in their methods as Miss
Grig, and Anson rarely found himself cornered.
By and by, too, the little flurry of curiosity
subsided, and it was not long before the neighbors had almost forgotten how " Dr. Bennett "
came by his title.   To this, however, they clung
with a tenacity which it was useless to combat.
How he hated it !   He used at first to feel as
though his friends were jeering at him when they
called him " doctor," and even in after years the
long-accustomed title would sometimes bring a
hot flush to his face.

Several years went by before pretty Alice Ives
was married, and then it was that Anson allowed
himself the one extravagance of his life.   He
went to the city and bought a water-color, for
which he paid more than he would have been
willing to admit.   The picture was not much appreciated in the community, but Alice liked it.
A branch of apple-blossoms against a pale blue
sky.   So exquisitely were they painted that even
the cavillers owned that you could almost smell
them, but " after all," they added, " it was nothing but a picture of apple-blossoms, just like
what anybody could see every spring, and you

would think it would be no great matter to paint a thing like that.''

Alice was so touched and pleased with the charming gift that she came over herself that same day after tea to thank Anson. It was June, and she found him working in his garden. She stepped lightly down the garden walk, clad in a flowered muslin, with a broad leghorn hat pushed back from her face. Anson did not see her com·ing. He was on his knees, weeding the border. Alice stood for a moment, watching him, and a wistful look came into her dark-blue eyes. Some-how he looked so poor in his old clothes and so lonesome, so different from the· Anson of a few years ago. There he knelt, pulling up the ugly weeds, and tossing them into a basket that stood beside him. She wished, vaguely, that he had been planting something. The sight of him gave her a heartache that she longed to ease. If she could only give him some little thing, just some-thing bright and sweet from her own abundance. She reached out her hand and plucked a spray of laburnum that grew beside the path. Yet no. It would be foolish to give him a flower out of his own garden, and she hastily tucked it into her bodice. Anson heard the sudden movement, and, turning, saw her standing there in the slanting sunlight. He got up and brushed the earth from his hands with his pocket-handkerchief, which he threw far away from him as Alice came toward him with outstretched hands.

"O Anson!" she cried, and in her voice there was a something that neither of them understood, a stray note of feeling which it was perhaps as well they should not understand. "O Anson! it is the loveliest of all my presents. How came you to think of giving me such a beautiful thing?"

"It came very natural," he answered, with an odd smile, as he took her hand in both his and looked down into the fair young face. "You always make me think of apple-blossoms, Alice."

ALICE.

VII

A NEW ENGLAND CONSCIENCE.

SEQUEL TO "A NEW ENGLAND QUACK."

THERE is a certain class of men who look like landmarks. No matter how slight may be their social importance, no matter how humble a part they may play in the active life of their town, they become identified with it. They are not necessarily men of marked appearance. It is only that a sight of one of them turning the key in his shop-door of an evening, or lingering about the church-porch after service, conveys a feeling of satisfaction. One's sense of the fitness of things is gratified, and one would rather see the bent figure and time-worn features than not.

Dr. Bennett belonged to this class of men. No more unobtrusive figure than his existed in the little manufacturing town of Westville. No citizen of the town went his ways more quietly than he. Yet his tall, stooping figure, his thin gray hair, his neat, threadbare coat, were clearly indigenous to the soil. His little shop, where he dealt in spectacles, magnifying-glasses, and kindred aids to vision, was as much a part of the landscape as the factory chimneys a few blocks away, or the ancient meeting-house round the corner. It had always been there, and as far as most people took the trouble to remember, it had always been presided over by Dr. Bennett.

His title was another thing about him which seemed an essential part of his personality, requiring no explanation. The fact that an optician is not usually called "doctor," rarely occurred to any one. There was no more curiosity about Dr. Bennett and his title than there was about the house he lived in, and the inappropriate cupola which perched on the gable-roof like a heavy barnyard fowl on a dove-cote. The cupola had emanated from the brain of Mrs. Henry Bennett, Dr. Bennett's mother, and if the truth were known, Anson Bennett's unearned title was also the outcome of that active-minded woman's ambition. It was she who had pushed her son into the practice of what she was pleased to call homœopathy, it was she who had watched with swelling pride and self-satisfaction his brilliant career, it was she who had never become reconciled to its abrupt close at the end of one winter's trial.

Something had happened, twenty-five years ago, to check the brilliant career of this only son, and he, who had formerly been so pliable in his mother's hands, had returned from the field of his country practice, a changed man. Something had happened to dash his youthful spirits, to kill his ambition, yet at the same time to harden and fix his character in new lines. It was not an unhappy love affair. None knew better than Jane Bennett that there was but one girl whom Anson had ever given a thought to, and she believed that that girl, the pretty Alice Ives, might have been his for the asking, long before she ever thought of marrying George Titcomb and going to live in Boston. No, if his love affair had ended disastrously, Anson had no one to thank for it but himself. Yet as he had deserted his new career in the full tide of success, Mrs. Bennett naturally found it impossible to credit his unvarnished statement that he had "made a botch of doctoring," and for that reason had come back to his old home and to his father's counter.

"You need n't talk to me," she had said over and over again to her meek good-humored spouse. "You need n't talk to me about Anson's not being a good doctor. 'T ain't likely he'd ha' made such a success of it if he had n't had the faculty. Why! Deacon Osgood says that his cousin on his mother's side, who lives jest out o' East Burnham, says they never was a doctor in those parts that everybody set such store by as Anson. That old fogy Dr. Morse had n't any show at all, long 's Anson stayed there. There 's something more at the bottom of it, you may depend upon it. I declare to goodness! when I see Anson moping round and sticking it out in that close-mouthed way, I 've half a mind to give him a good shaking!"

"I wish you would!" Henry Bennett would answer, with suppressed amusement, "I should jest like to see you!"

The idea of her husband's making a joke at her expense would not have found easy entrance into Jane Bennett's mind. She never dreamed that, as he made this harmless remark, he was conjuring up a picture of the scene. She was a small woman, to be sure, and her son, in those early days, was a tall, muscular man. But so strong was her sense of maternal authority that no exercise of it seemed incongruous. Had she suspected that her mild-visaged husband, whom she had always domineered over, and consequently looked down upon, knew the whole story of his son's misadventure, her indignation would have known no bounds. It was well for the peace of all concerned that no such suspicion ever crossed her mind.

Meanwhile a quarter of a century had passed over Jane Bennett, and the disappointment of her life. Kind deprecatory Henry Bennett, had long since received his last conjugal snub, had long since had his last sly chuckle at his wife's expense, and very quietly, as was his nature, he had slipped out of the matrimonial bonds, by the only loophole of escape open to such as he.

At the end of that quarter of a century, Jane

Bennett's figure was as alert and as wiry as ever; her hair was as black, her glance as sharp. Time's chisel had not been keen enough to do much execution on that resolute countenance. All the deeper had been its marks upon her son's face. At the age of fifty, Anson Bennett looked older, duller, wearier than his mother.

This especially when his face was in repose, as was usually the case, and never more so than when undergoing a remonstrance from his mother.

They were sitting together at dinner one Sunday noon in November. Mrs. Bennett behind her cold joint, looking precisely as Anson remembered her from his earliest childhood. Not that the fashion of her dress or of her surroundings had remained unchanged. Mrs. Bennett prided herself not a little upon her modishness. A plain white china service had, in accordance with the fashion of the day, superseded the old blue stoneware, which, with its Dutch canal views and inconsequent minarets, had been the delight of Anson's childhood; an elaborate plated-silver caster adorned the middle of the table; while on the wall opposite him a many-hued chromo had taken the place of the two cheap companion prints once dear to his heart. Yet amid all these changes his mother's face seemed to him quite unaltered, and the voice in which she did her fault-finding was the same voice at whose sound he had trembled before he learned to recognize any higher authority than that of its owner.

11

"I must say, Anson," said the sharp voice, "I must say that I was mortified to see you going to church this morning in your old winter overcoat. When I 've been at you for a month o' Sundays about getting a new one. Why on earth do you keep putting it off?"

"I don't want a new overcoat," said Anson, quietly.

"You don't want a new overcoat? Well, you 'd ought to be ashamed of yourself if you don't. That 's all I can say. They was n't a man in the middle aisle that looked as shabby as you did. If I was you I 'd try and scare up a little self-respect jest for the sake of appearances."

"The overcoat 's as warm as it ever was," said Anson, slowly and stubbornly. "And what I want an overcoat for is warmth. When I begin to feel cold in it I 'll get another."

"Yes! and till it lets the wind through, you 'll go about looking like what folks call you—an old miser!"

Jane Bennett shot a sidewise glance at her son, to note the effect of the word. To her chagrin it had apparently no effect whatever. Dr. Bennett ate his dinner with unimpaired relish, and looked ready for a change of subject. The son sat at the side of the table, and not opposite his mother, as would have seemed natural. It was characteristic of Anson, though few credited him with the finer sensibilities, that he never had been able to overcome his reluctance to taking his father's seat at table. He had at first feared to hurt his mother's feelings by so doing, and when at last it dawned upon him that his father's widow was not sensitive in such matters, a new compunction and loyalty took possession of him, and from that time forward he guarded the old man's memory with jealous tenderness.

To-day, as his mother chid him, for she did not let the subject rest there, his mind wandered, as it often did, to the kind old man whose plain sense of duty had sustained him when duty was not easy. In a flash of memory he beheld the changes which had passed over his father's face when he had come to him in the crisis of his life. The incredulity, and then the pain, with which the elder man had listened as his son told him how, in his ignorance and presumption, he had undoubtedly caused the death of a patient ; the relief with which his listener learned that he should give up the practice of medicine, though in so doing he was giving up a distinction which had been the pride of Henry Bennett's heart. Best of all, the glow of approval in the homely old face, the quick tears in the kind eyes, when Anson declared his intention of undertaking the support of this same James Ellery's family.

But while all this passed in Anson Bennett's mind his face wore the look his mother best knew —a look of quiet obstinacy—a look which exasperated her. And it came to pass, as it often did

in their one-sided discussions, that Jane Bennett's
wish to carry her point was overborne by a desire
to punish her son. As she gave him a second
"help" of boiled potatoes, she asked, with apparent irrelevancy :

"Did you see Alice Ives that was ? She was
sitting in her Pa's pew, dressed up real stylish
and becomin'. I thought when I saw her looking at you across the aisle that she must be glad
enough that she 'd had the sense to marry a man
that was free with his money."

"No, I did n't see Alice," said Anson, calmly.
He did not flush nor wince, nor did his voice
betray any emotion. Yet a change went over his
countenance, something like the change which
goes over a dull landscape when the long afternoon light begins to brood.

"I 'm glad Alice is so well off," he added,
presently. "They say she 's got two little girls
as pretty as she used to be."

"She 's jest as pretty as ever she was," said
his mother, sharply. "I do hope to goodness,"
she added, "that you wont go to see her in that
old overcoat. She 's going away to-morrow."

"I don't know 's I shall go to see her at all,"
he answered. "At any rate, I 'm going over to
East Burnham this afternoon to see Dr. Morse."

Poor Jane Bennett had got the worst of it, as
she often did nowadays. Dr. Morse was her bugbear. Without ever having seen that excellent
man, she had conceived an aversion to him which

was perhaps not without foundation. In the first place, he was an "allopath," and although her son had kept his allegiance to homœopathy, maintaining that he had "made a botch of doctoring" only because he was totally ignorant of the whole subject of medicine, although she could not accuse Dr. Morse of having converted her son to his own views, yet she knew by intuition that he had in some way been instrumental in the downfall of her ambition. Furthermore, the fact that the only indulgence Anson ever permitted himself was an occasional visit to the doctor at East Burnham, was in itself enough to excite her jealousy. What had this old fogy to do with her boy? what attraction could he have to offer? At first she had fancied there might be a daughter in the case; that perhaps Anson, faithless to his first love, had lost his heart to one of the Miss Morses; that he had relinquished doctoring to please the old man. But all her speculations had come to nought, and now she had nothing more definite in support of her aversion than the same instinctive distrust which she had always cherished. And so it happened that when Anson said he was going to East Burnham his mother felt peculiarly frustrated, and she wondered in her heart what she had ever done to deserve so undutiful a son. It was true that he had always treated her with scrupulous justice, that she enjoyed her fair share of his business profits, that with all his alleged miserliness he paid his board regularly, that he never spoke a disrespectful word to her, but all this had little weight. Jane Bennett took her blessings for granted. Her mind dwelt by preference upon her small vexations.

Yet if she had her faults, and no one could deny them, the poor woman endured her full measure of punishment. Faults of disposition are not as grave as many of those to which human nature is heir, but they bring their own retribution. And while Jane Bennett alienated her son's affection by a course of steady opposition, of daily bickering, yet there was nothing which she craved as she did that very filial love which got no chance to blossom.

Perhaps she was in reality more sinned against than sinning. Certainly, when Anson, twenty-five years previous, had refrained from telling her the true story of the disaster which had fallen upon him, he had done her a cruel injustice. The fact, too, that her husband had had no impulse to take her into his confidence showed that he also misjudged her. In spite of her narrow-mindedness, her self-conceit, her ill-temper, Jane Bennett had very strict ideas of right and wrong. If she once had been convinced that Anson had committed a wrong, even at her own instigation, she would have been eager to see the wrong atoned for. As it was, she lived in a tangle of vexations, to which she had no clue. How could she know that her son's life was one long expiation? How could she divine that he wore his shabby old clothes and walked in a narrow, monotonous path in order that he might fulfil what he felt to be a sacred duty? Living herself in a state of chronic disappointment and chagrin, she badgered her son into a dull indifference, and underneath her apparent self-confidence was a mortifying and wounding conviction that he did not love her.

When Anson returned from East Burnham that same evening, he did not go directly home. He went to his shop instead, closed the door behind him, lighted the gas, and fell to tinkering a pair of glasses that had been left with him for repairs. It was not the first time that he had sought refuge from unruly emotions in the exercise of his prosaic calling, but it was the first time that he had done so of a Sunday evening. He reflected, however, that his grandmother, Old Lady Pratt, always kept her Sabbath from sundown to sundown, and that what was a principle with her could not be a crime in her grandson. And so he worked away as industriously as though his daily bread had depended upon the immediate completion of that small job.

Meanwhile his face looked younger, happier, more animated, than it had looked for years, and no one seeing it would have guessed the nature of the errand from which he had just returned. He had gone that afternoon to consult his old friend upon his own condition; he had learned that certain strange and disturbing sensations he had experienced of late were the symptoms of a malignant disease from which nothing but a severe surgical operation could possibly save him. He knew that the result of such an operation was very doubtful, yet he had determined to entrust his case to a young surgeon, James Ellery by name, whose education and opening career he had watched with an intense interest, the secret of which only Dr. Morse knew. James Ellery, the youngest of the five children left fatherless through Anson Bennett's fault, had shown an aptitude for study, and Anson had joyfully undertaken to educate the boy for the practice of medicine. Now at last the boy had grown to be a man, fully equipped for his profession, giving promise of unusual distinction, and Anson Bennett's heart was far more bound up in this young career than in his own colorless, eventless life. As he sat tinkering the old glasses a feeling of exultation made his heart beat faster. Yes, he, Anson Bennett, had been the determining power in this young man's life. Unaware though he was, of the very name of his benefactor, young Ellery owed his education, owed his future to him, the wretched quack, on whose ignorant ambition his father had been sacrificed. And now Dr. Morse saw no reason why this boy should not undertake to perform one of the most difficult operations known to science, and he, Anson Bennett, was to furnish the test.

The town clock struck nine, and Anson put up his tools and prepared to leave the shop. As he

ANSON.

stepped out into the night air, he found himself taking a round-about way home. It was prettier by way of High Street, he said to himself, but in his heart he knew that it was the presence of his old love in the ancient square house behind the elm trees, that lured his feet from the usual path.

It was a bleak November evening. The wind swayed the bare branches of the trees in front of the old Ives homestead. A fragile-looking moon, about a week old, was pitching and tossing among the clouds, and Anson vaguely wondered if it might not founder. There were lights in several of the windows, and he paused a moment, looking at them. He did not speculate as to Alice's whereabouts in the house. Rather, he had a feeling that all that soft, curtained light emanated from her presence. And as he stood there he recalled the day, the very hour, in which he had last thought of her as a possible possession of his own. He remembered the exact appearance of the horse he was driving that day, the creaking of the wheel of his chaise, causing him to wonder whether he was going to have a hot box ; he remembered how green were the meadows between which he drove, and most clearly, most poignantly did he recall the rich scent of the apple-blossoms, the peculiar delicacy of their color, and the way a stray petal came floating down and rested on his knee. To-night there was no longer any pain in these recollections. He seemed to be losing hold of his old

self and his old desires, and even as he stood
before the house, whose roof sheltered Alice, his
mind returned with a sudden rebound to the
thought of what was coming, and he hurried
home with a quick step and a light heart.

In the few days that intervened before the operation was performed, Dr. Bennett led his usual
life, maintained all his usual habits. Every
morning he walked in his shabby old overcoat to
his little shop, where he industriously mended
old glasses, or made an occasional sale of new
ones. When meal-times came, he sat at table
with his mother, and patiently answered her
questions, letting her talk and speculate, criticise
and suggest what she would in regard to the impending event. But though he never failed in
attention to her words, he was singularly oblivious to the signs of anxiety and distress in her
face and manner, which would not have escaped
an ordinary observer. If he gave a thought to
the matter, it was merely to note that she seemed
more irritable than usual. He never guessed the
tension of feeling under which she was living.

Once he said a very cruel thing to her. It was
at breakfast two days before the Thursday which
mother and son looked forward to with such different feelings. Anson did not notice the lines
and shadows on his mother's face which beto-
kened a sleepless night, nor did he dream that she
had lain awake hour after hour, wondering what
she could do to express her love and solicitude.

" Anson," she said, looking not at him, but at a hole in her napkin, which she seemed to have just discovered, " Anson, I.'ve been thinking that I 'd *give* you a new overcoat this winter, seeing as you don't care to buy one."

With that singular obtuseness where his mother was concerned, which had grown upon this good and conscientious man, he fancied that she only meant to shame him into doing as she wished, and he said, indifferently :

" I guess you 'd better not, Mother. I may not need an overcoat after Thursday."

She was in the act of passing him his coffee, and her hand shook so that the saucer was quite flooded. Anson emptied the contents of the saucer back into the cup, suppressing his annoyance. He hated to have his coffee slopped, but he never found fault with his mother. He had the reputation of being a very considerate son.

They made up a bed for him in the little old sitting-room, where most of the evenings of his life had been spent. And his chief feeling, as he laid himself down upon the bed, was one of regret that he was not to be allowed to retain his consciousness, and be a witness to the skill of his young surgeon. He watched him with the greatest interest before the ether was administered. He liked the precision of the young man's movements, the clearness of his glance, the unobtrusive self-confidence of his manner. He heard Dr. Morse ask his mother to leave the room, and his eyes did not follow her retreating figure, nor did he see the look she gave him as she turned away.

An hour later three figures sat beside the bed, waiting for signs of returning consciousness. Dr. Morse, his gray head bent and his shaggy eyebrows meeting, regarded the patient with calm watchfulness. The glance and attitude of the young physician were intense and eager. On the other side of the bed, close to the wall, sat a small, erect figure ; the face, with a pinched look on it, showing sharp-cut against the wall-paper, on which gaily dressed shepherdesses smirked and courtesied. Jane Bennett's sharp black eyes were fixed upon the closed lids of her son. When Anson moved slightly, as he did several times before the lids were raised, she started eagerly forward ; but when at last he opened his eyes, it was toward his old friend that they were turned.

"Well, Doctor," he said, in a feeble voice, " how did the operation go ? "

" Splendidly," said Dr. Morse. " Splendidly ! But don't exert yourself to talk."

With a look of perfect content the sick man closed his eyes.

For many hours Anson seemed to be sleeping peacefully. Yet to the mother's perception, no less than to the trained eye of the physician, it was clear that his life was ebbing.

The day wore away and night came on, and still the two men watched beside him ; and still that small rigid figure kept guard between the bed and the pictured shepherdesses. Once or twice the doctors asked some service of her, which she performed swiftly and exactly, after which she slipped back to her disregarded post.

Just after midnight Anson opened his eyes once more, and smiled faintly. Dr. Morse bent toward him.

" Bennett," he said, with a compassionate look toward the mother, " Bennett, this has been a great strain upon your system. It is only fair to tell you that it is possible that you may not pull through."

" Tell me again," the patient questioned, " was there anything wrong about the operation ? "

" The operation was magnificent," his friend declared, " but you don't seem to have the vitality you need."

"That's no account, Doctor, that's no account." The dying man's voice was almost querulous. " The *operation's* the thing. That's all we care about."

Then turning to Ellery he added, half apologetically : " You see, Doctor, I once did a little doctoring myself, and I've kept up my interest in these things."

His mother put her hand on his, and he looked at her wonderingly.

" Why, mother," he said. " You up so late? Had n't you better go to bed ? "

Toward morning he rallied once more, and signed to Ellery to come nearer. The young man bent a grave face to listen.

"Dr. Ellery," said Bennett slowly. "Don't you worry because you 've lost a patient. You 've done your part magnificently. Did n't you hear Dr. Morse say so? Magnificently! And he 's a good judge—I tell you—he 's—a—good—judge."

His voice wavered a little on these last words, as though the thought were eluding him. His mind had evidently wandered.

And Jane Bennett, whose self-assertion had never before failed her, only sat there, with a piteous, drawn look about her lips, her eyes fixed upon the tranquil face which did not turn toward hers. Dr. Morse had grasped the patient's hand, and bent down to hear what he might say. The sick man's eyes were open, and there was a strange, remote look in them. Suddenly a change came, his face lighted up, and he whispered eagerly:

"See! See! Apple-blossoms!" And with their fragrance on his spirit, Anson Bennett died.

Then, too late to reach his ears, a voice sharp with agony cried:

"Anson! O Anson! You forgot your mother!"

VIII

THE SCHOOLMARM.

A DISAGREEABLE sensation was caused throughout the entire Pratt family when Mary William announced her intention of "keeping school." Old Lady Pratt, who knew the history of the family ever since she came into it, some sixty years before, could testify that no daughter of that highly respectable house had ever "worked for a living." An unprejudiced observer might have thought that Old Lady Pratt herself had worked for a living, and worked harder than any school-teacher, all through the childhood of her six boys and girls. But that, of course, was a different matter, as anybody must understand. A woman toiling early and late for husband and children was but fulfilling the chief end and aim of her being, but a woman who set out to wrest a living from the world, when she "need want for nothing at home," was clearly flying in the face of Providence.

"Well, Mary," she said to her grand-daughter, "you must not expect me to countenance any such step."

" Why not, Grandma ? "

" Why not? Because I don't approve of young women gettin' dissatisfied with the sphere to which they 've been called. That 's why not."

" But I have n't been called to any sphere. Now that Bessie and Willie are almost as grown up as I am, mother does n't need me any more, and I don't see why I 'm not entitled to a change if I want one."

" If you want a change," said Grandma, promptly ; "you 'd much better get married."

" Now, Grandma ! You know well enough that I never had an offer. If I had, you 'd have heard of it fast enough."

" And you don't deserve to have one," cried the old lady, with asperity, "if you go and *spile* everything by turning schoolmarm."

This was a sore subject with Old Lady Pratt. She, who was the sworn foe to single blessedness, had constantly to hear that her own granddaughters had "never had an offer." It was not that they were less sought than other girls of their age, but early marriages had almost gone out of fashion since Grandma's day, and many a handsome girl might get to be well on in the twenties before a serious suitor made his appearance.

Mary William—so called to distinguish her from her Uncle Anson's daughter, who went by the name of Mary Anson—Mary William was at this time twenty-one years of age. Her father, the

hero of the family, had been killed at the first battle of Bull Run, six years previous. He had left
his affairs, what there was of them, in such perfect order that his widow knew precisely what she
had to depend upon—a fact on which all the Pratts
laid great emphasis. But to know one's financial
status, if that status chance to be extremely low,
is scarcely compensation for hardships and priva-
tions, and Mrs. William Pratt used fervently to
wish that there had been just sufficient inaccuracy
in her husband's accounts to leave a margin of
possibility that a windfall might yet occur.

Mrs. William Pratt was not a woman of much
energy or resource. She had a few fixed ideas,
one of them being that she could not consent to
"come down in the world." Coming down in
the world meant to her comprehension renting or
selling the commodious, well-built house in which
her husband had installed her during the days of
their prosperity, and moving into smaller quarters. Her house was Edna Pratt's special pride.
It was large and rambling, with a front hall
which did not confine itself to the manifest mis-
sion of furnishing a landing-place from the stairs,
but spread itself out into an octagonal space,
wherein pillars stood supporting arches; a dim
ancestral-looking hall, which could not fail to
impress a stranger. But as strangers rarely visited
Mrs. William Pratt, and as nearly all the frequenters of the house distinctly remembered its
erection a dozen or more years previous, the hall

12

did not make quite the baronial impression which might have been expected. Mary William, especially when performing the arduous duties of maid-of-all-work minus the wages, used to murmur within herself against the hall, and against all the spacious rooms, which seemed to have taken their cue from it. For she reflected that every superfluous square yard of floor meant just so much more carpet to sweep ; that every inch of wood-work offered just so much more of a resting-place for dust. Mary William was of the opinion that her youth had been deliberately sacrificed to the house, and pre-eminently to the pillared hall, and she secretly rebelled against it with all her might and main. Not work for her living, indeed ? How many a time had the one "girl" of the establishment been dismissed on some slight pretext ! How many a time had her "place" remained vacant, and while Mrs. William Pratt sat in the parlor or lingered among the baronial pillars, complaining to visitors of the inferiority and scarcity of servants, the unfortunate Mary William had stood scorching her face over the kitchen stove, or cleaning the set of elaborate *repoussé* silver, which lent such an air of distinction to their sideboard.

But Mary William was a young person of much determination and rather unusual intelligence, and while her hands grew rough and her temper just a little sharpened in the drudgery of her daily life, she saw to it that no rust should gather upon her excellent mental faculties. She had graduated from the high-school at the head of her class, and after her education was thus "completed," she managed with the aid of the public library, to do a good deal of solid reading and some studying. Mary William was not intended for a bookworm, but she turned to books as being the most congenial and the least exacting society within her reach. She was not able to dress well and tastefully. She was not able to entertain her friends at home, being far too poor for such luxuries. Neither was she the girl to enjoy playing a subordinate part in life, and she felt keenly the social disabilities which her poverty imposed upon her. She had never been of a complaining disposition, and no one suspected her of any discontent with her lot. But in her own mind she had long contemplated a declaration of independence, to be made when she should come of age. This was to occur in July, but she had no intention of hurrying matters. When she came down to breakfast, however, on the very morning of her twenty-first birthday, she suddenly found it impossible to refrain from making known her plans.

"Teach school!" cried her mother, in a tone of ineffectual protest.

"Be a schoolmarm!" cried Bessie; while Willie, who was still subject to the redoubtable race of schoolmarms, gazed upon her with a mixture of awe and incredulity.

"I never heard of such a ridiculous idea," said Mrs. William Pratt.

"I don't see anything ridiculous about it," Mary retorted, giving vent to her feelings with unprecedented freedom. "I've been scrimping and pinching and slaving all my life, and now I want to try how it feels to have a few dollars of my own."

"A few dollars of your own!" cried her mother. "Why, Mary, what an ungrateful girl you are! Does n't your Aunt Harriet give you twenty-five dollars every single birthday?"

"Yes, Aunt Harriet is very kind; but twenty-five dollars is n't what you would call an ample income."

"But you have more than that to spend, and your living not costing you a cent either!"

"No; neither does her living cost Bridget a cent"; and then Mary William stopped, and did not pursue the comparison, an act of forbearance which should be recorded to her credit.

After breakfast sixteen-year-old Bessie came up to her with wondering eyes, and said, "Mary, do you suppose you 'll get rich teaching school?"

"Not very rich, puss."

"I wish there were some way of getting rich, don't you?"

"Indeed I do, Bessie."

"What would you do, Mary, if you were rich?"

"I should sail for Europe next week; and I should send Willie to college when it came time."

" And me ? "

" You ? " said Mary, looking thoughtfully at her pretty little sister. " I would give you every single thing you wanted."

This feeling for Bessie, that she was a creature born to have every wish gratified, was common to all who knew the child. Mary had no fear that in the event of her leaving home she should shift the burden of household drudgery on to her younger sister's shoulders. Even Mrs. William Pratt would not have made Bessie work.

Now Mrs. William Pratt, though a weak woman, and both vain and selfish, was much respected in her husband's family. All were grateful to her for having kept up appearances on so small an income, and the fact that this had been done at her daughter Mary's expense was not wholly understood, even by her sharp-eyed mother-in-law. Hence, when she raised a cry of indignation at Mary's revolutionary behavior, she was sustained by a full chorus of disapproval from the whole clan.

Nevertheless Mary carried her point. Her venture was successful beyond her hopes. She had not led her class in the high school for nothing. No sooner had she made known her intentions than she was offered the position of assistant in the grammar-school of her own district, with the munificent salary of $350.

Singularly enough, her actual engagement as a teacher wrought an entire change in the feelings of the family. It was like the first plunge into cold water. The family pride had shrunk from it, but a reaction set in almost immediately, and that same family pride experienced a glow of gratification that one of their number should be so capable and so well thought of. Small as was the sum which Mary was to receive for her services, it was relatively large—large measured by her previous limitations. Her more prosperous relatives had become so accustomed to the extremely small income which the William Pratts had to live upon that they had come to regard it as quite in the natural order of things, and to bear it with philosophical indifference. Now, however, that Mary had taken matters into her own hands, and was prepared to mould her own fortunes, they rejoiced with her as loudly as though they had hitherto realized her deprivations.

Old Lady Pratt alone withheld her approval. The fact of Mary's having a little more money seemed to her to be of small consequence in comparison with the girl's "prospects." She was made of sterner stuff than her descendants; she knew deprivation and hard work by heart, and she was not in the least afraid of them for herself or for anybody else. Even when Mrs. William Pratt told her that Mary had offered to pay three dollars a week for the "girl's" wages, Old Lady Pratt remained obdurate.

"Nonsense, Edna!" she said, sharply. "It would n't hurt you a mite to do your own work.

You 'd a sight better do it than to have Mary
turn out an old maid. There 's Eliza Pelham,
now. She acted jest so' when she was Mary's
age, and she 'll teach school to the end of the
chapter. She got so set in her ways and so high-
flyin' in her notions that the Gov'nor himself
would n't have suited her. You mark my words,
Mary 'll be an old maid, jest like Eliza. You see
'f she ain't.''

And if Mary herself had been asked, she would
have been the first to admit the reasonableness of
her grandmother's predictions. She had never
been so happy in her life as she was the day on
which she stepped upon the platform at school
and assumed the responsibilities of " schoolmarm." Mary William loved to teach, and she
loved also to rule—an art which she understood
to perfection. There were some pretty black
sheep among her flock, but before she had had
them a month they had learned a lesson in
wholesome discipline which seemed to them
much more incontrovertible than anything Murray had to say against alliances between plural
subjects and singular verbs, or any of Greenleaf's
arithmetical theories. The new teacher's success
made so strong an impression upon the school
committee that by Christmas-time Miss Pratt's
name was mentioned in connection with a $500
vacancy to occur the coming year in the high-
school. Meanwhile Mary revelled in her independence ; and if she thought of matrimony in

connection with herself, it was as a state of bondage to be avoided at any cost.

One pleasant day in April the young teacher had just dismissed a class in compound fractions, and sat looking down upon the motley collection of boys and girls arranged with geometrical symmetry over the large room. She was aware of a spirit of restlessness among them. There were more boys than usual engaged in the time-honored custom of twisting their legs in intricate patterns about the legs of their chairs, more girls gazing dreamily at the budding tree-tops just visible through the high windows. Mary knew by her own uneven pulse that the seeds were sprouting in the ground outside, and that the spring trouble was stirring in the veins of all that youthful concourse. Mary William was in some respects wise beyond her years, and she did not reprove the vagaries of boyish legs and girlish eyes. But she kept a careful watch upon them during the study hour which preceded the long noon recess.

Just before twelve o'clock she was surprised by the entrance of two well-dressed ladies who did not look quite like products of Dunbridge soil. As she went forward to meet them they called her by name, the more stately of the two introducing herself as Mrs. Beardsley, of Stanton. Mary William, though somewhat mystified, bàde her guests welcome with a very good grace, saying that she was on the point of dismissing the school.

The dispersion of the fifty or more boys and

THE SCHOOLMARM.

girls was a matter of some ceremony—a ceremony
regulated by a succession of strokes on the teacher's bell, and usually very strictly observed. At
a certain critical point in the proceedings to-day,
of all days of the year, the boys broke loose, and
made a stampede for the door, the girls remaining
in the aisles, with their arms crossed behind them
—models of propriety before company. Mary
William's face flushed brightly, and she struck
the shrill bell three times in rapid succession.
Instantly the rabble of unruly boys stood trans-
fixed. Two or three of them who had already
escaped into the sunshine came sneaking back at
the peremptory summons, while Mary William's
voice, with a bell-like ring in it, said : " Boys,
return to your seats ! "

When all the boys' seats were filled with more
or less contrite occupants, the order of exercises
was resumed on the part of the girls, who filed
quietly out of the room. Then Mary turned to
her guests in a disengaged manner, with the assurance that she was quite at their service. A
momentous conversation ensued.

Mrs. Beardsley stated that she was the Mrs.
Beardsley whose school for young ladies had so
long maintained its reputation as the leading
school for young ladies in the state. Miss Pratt
had doubtless heard of Mrs. Beardsley's school
for young ladies. Miss Pratt was very sorry, but
she was totally ignorant of any young ladies'
school whatever outside her own town.

Mary had the discrimination to perceive that Mrs. Beardsley was a thorough woman of the world, and that she thought extremely well of herself. Nevertheless, she listened with entire self-possession to the revelations which followed.

Mrs. Beardsley was in search of a teacher to fill the place in the coming year of a valued assistant about to retire. She had heard Miss Pratt well spoken of by her cousin, the Rev. Mr. Ingraham, of Dunbridge, and she had come, with her sister, Miss Ingraham, to interview Miss Pratt. Miss Pratt signified her willingness to be interviewed, asking permission at the same time to dismiss the culprits, whose durance she considered to have been sufficiently long. This time the dispersion was performed with a precision which an army sergeant might have envied. As the door closed behind the last round jacket, Mrs. Beardsley resumed the thread of her discourse :

" My requirements, Miss Pratt, are somewhat severe. My school has a reputation to sustain, which necessitates rather exceptional qualifications in my assistants. The sort of discipline, for instance, which you have just carried out so successfully with those rough boys, would be entirely out of place in a school whose members are young ladies from the first families in the state. Tact and worldly wisdom are essential in the government of such a body. Having no doubt of your acquirements as a mere teacher of the branches desired—namely, Latin and mathematics—I am disposed to dwell more especially upon my exactions of a social nature. A teacher in my school must have the good-breeding and the equanimity of a lady, and, pardon my suggestion, she must dress in perfect taste.''

Mary flushed slightly, being conscious of the ugliness of her gown, which had descended to her from a cousin whose means exceeded her discretion in matters of taste.

Mrs. Beardsley, having paused a moment, that the full weight of her words might take effect, asked, "Do you feel, Miss Pratt, that you are fitted in every particular to fill such a position ? "

The flush on Mary's face had subsided, and to her own surprise she did not flinch. She raised her clear hazel eyes to those of her catechist, and with a direct gaze, in which there was unmistakable power, she said, quietly, "Yes, Mrs. Beardsley, I do.''

Mrs. Beardsley returned the girl's look with an accession of interest. The "woman of the world'' was not a creature of impulse, but she was a student of character, and, without a moment's hesitation, she said, "I engage you.''

"Thank you,'' said the new assistant, as though the conversation were ended.

Mrs. Beardsley and Miss Ingraham exchanged glances, and waited for Mary's next remark; but it was not forthcoming. Mary seemed for the moment to have forgotten herself. She was looking about the homely room where she had served her short apprenticeship, lost in wonder over her sudden good fortune. Mary William was deeply impressed by Mrs. Beardsley's personality. She had always wanted to have a taste of the "great world." She loved the amenities of life, she loved the power which social training gives, and to her unsophisticated mind it seemed as though a school presided over by Mrs. Beardsley—a school where were gathered the daughters of the "first families in the state"—must offer an opening through which she might get at least a peep into that same great world.

Finding her future assistant disinclined to take the initiative, Mrs. Beardsley said, "You have asked me nothing about terms, Miss Pratt."

"Oh yes! Terms!" answered Mary William, recalled to practical affairs, in which she felt no sentimental lack of interest.

"That is, of course, in a certain sense, my affair," Mrs. Beardsley resumed ; "but I should be curious to know your ideas on the subject."

Mary looked at her shrewdly. "I suppose the salary would be proportionate to the requirements," she said.

"A very reasonable supposition," Mrs. Beardsley admitted. "Then we will come to the point. As only a small number of my pupils live in my family, I shall not require your services there. You will, therefore, be at some expense for your living, and I had thought of offering you "—she paused a moment to notice whether the girl

looked eager, but Mary William gave no sign—
"twelve hundred and fifty dollars. Should you
think that a fair compensation?"

Mary's eyes sparkled. Touched by the generosity of such an offer to a mere grammar-school
teacher, she cried, impulsively, "I ought to be a
better teacher than I am, to be worth all that to
you."

Mrs. Beardsley was gratified, but she only said,
"If you are not worth that, you are worth
nothing to me."

Mrs. Beardsley had gone out in search of a
"treasure," and she had found one. As for
Mary William, she had set forth on an errand
almost as humble as Saul's, and, like him, she
suddenly found herself endowed—to her own
thinking—with a kingdom.

All summer long Mary spent much of her time
in fashioning tasteful garments, wherein to meet
one, at least, of Mrs. Beardsley's requirements,
and her needle went in and out as gayly as though
set to music.

Her friends told her of proposed journeyings or
weeks to be spent at the seaside, but she envied
none of them. What were a few weeks of pleas-
uring compared to the gift of liberty to live
your own life in your own way? As she tried on
one completed garment after another, examining
the effect critically in the glass, she thought of
Mrs. Beardsley and of that formidable band of
school-girls, and she took heart of hope.

One day she stood before her mirror, arrayed in a claret-colored cashmere, which was to be her "Sunday gown" in the coming winter. There was a trimming of velvet ribbon which was highly effective, and the broad tatting collar was very becoming to the round white throat within it. Mary studied the dress with some satisfaction, and then she inadvertently looked up at her reflected face. For the first time in her life she was struck with her own good looks, and her eyes danced with pleasure. Mrs. Beardsley would be more likely to approve her, the school-girls would perhaps like her, if she looked like that. She smiled at herself, and the pretty teeth thus revealed added greatly to the favorable impression.

"How absurd I am!" she said to herself, and she laughed aloud. She had never seen her laughing face before. It had been a prematurely serious countenance which she had associated with herself. "Oh, is n't it delicious to be alive?" she exclaimed, confidingly, to her own image.

If vanity is pleasure in one's own good points, Mary William was rapidly developing her share of it. But the beauty and originality of her vanity consisted in the turn it took. It looked only to pleasing a middle-aged woman and a school full of young girls, and, as such well-regulated vanity deserved, it was crowned with success.

The first week in September—for schools began earlier in Mary William's day than in ours—Mrs. Beardsley's "treasure" arrived upon the scene, and took all hearts by storm. It would be difficult to say whether the exhilaration of her spirits made the new teacher charming, or whether her almost instant popularity was the secret of that same exhilaration. Such things go hand in hand. Certain it is that Mary William lived in a round of pleasures far more stimulating, and far more satisfying too, than the pleasures usually thus designated. She loved her work so thoroughly that its very difficulties but lent it zest. She liked the girls, and she regarded Mrs. Beardsley with the enthusiastic devotion felt by a subaltern for his superior officer.

And so the first school term went by only too swiftly, and the long Christmas vacation came as an unwelcome interruption. How much more unwelcome would it have been had Mary William known what it held in store for her! Nothing could have been more unlooked for, nothing could have been to Mary more unwished for, than the events which followed upon the arrival from his Western ranch of the minister's son, Fred Ingraham. When Mary returned home for the holidays, he had been in Dunbridge scarcely a week, and had not yet ceased to be the sensation of the hour.

Fred Ingraham came into her life with all the freshness and insistency of a prairie breeze, which

goes sweeping across level leagues unhindered by
any obstacle, unabashed by any contrary currents.
This minister's son, with his high-bred features
and his air of conscious power, belonged to the
finest type of ranchman. In him many of the
best qualities springing from the old civilization
existed side by side with the spirit and vigor
which animate the pioneer. There was not lacking a touch of the absolute monarch, such as your
genuine ranchman was five-and-twenty years ago.
Being, then, a young man of ready decision and
of hitherto unalterable determination, no sooner
did he behold the little girl whom he had patronized in big-boy fashion a few years previous,
transformed into a surprising likeness to his
secretly-cherished ideal of a woman, than he fell
precipitately in love with her. There was no
time to be lost in preliminaries, and Fred pressed
his suit with the courage and persistency which
might have been expected of an absolute monarch
—to say nothing of a Yankee boy accustomed to
deal with rough cowboys and pitching bronchos.

Mary was at first thrown off her guard by the
very suddenness of the assault. She had been
predisposed in his favor by all she knew of the
daring and independence of his course in breaking loose from family traditions and choosing his
own rough path in life. She looked upon him as
a kindred spirit, and they had many a long talk
and more than one walk together in the sparkling
Christmas weather before she took the alarm.

He had often talked to her of ranch life—so new and interesting a theme in those early days, before the cowboy had been tamed into print. He told her of the life of adventure and hardship which he had known, of his vast herds of cattle, and his wide domains. It seemed to her as though this dominion over men and over beasts had conferred upon him a certain patent of nobility, and she listened with kindling attention to all he had to say. But if he seemed to her to be something of a hero, it was the hero of a realm as remote from her as were the lands of the Orient or the ages of the past. And because of the remoteness and foreignness of her interest hitherto, because of her perfect sense of aloofness from it all, she had listened without suspicion or constraint.

They were walking home together from the skating pond one afternoon, their two pairs of skates rattling gayly together in her companion's hand, making a pleasant metallic accompaniment to his narration.

Suddenly he interrupted himself to say: "Mary, you would like ranch life immensely. I am sure of it. Don't you think you would?"

His words were harmless enough, but the sudden pleading urgency of his manner, and something new and intensely personal in his tone, startled her, and she instantly bristled.

"Oh, yes!" she said. "I've no doubt I should like it if I were a man. But it must be a hideous life for a woman."

13

Fred bore the rebuff manfully, though it felt as grating and as blinding as a sudden prairie sand-storm. He turned and looked at her as she walked erect and strong by his side. A more defiant-looking young person he had never seen, nor a more altogether desirable one. Good heavens! the very curve of her chin was worth dying for, and Fred drew a deep breath and swore within himself that she should yet be vanquished.

The rest of that day Mary tried vainly to be-lieve that her panic had been foolish and uncalled for. But she knew better. She feared that it was unmaidenly and conceited; that she was de-serving of all the worst epithets usually applied to a forward girl; but she knew as positively as though Fred had told her so in plain English that this remarkably strong-willed young man was planning to overturn her whole scheme of life, to wrest from her her precious independence, to make her life subordinate to his. She would not allow herself to think in terms less harsh of his designs, and she put herself on the defensive in a manner so transparent that it would have been amusing to any one less immediately inter-ested in her state of mind than Fred.

He meanwhile did his best to retrieve that first blunder by the exercise of an almost superhuman discretion. He saw his opportunity slipping away with the fleeting vacation days; he knew that in a cruelly short time Mary would be once

more intrenched in her beloved work under the
protection of that much-respected dragon Mrs.
Beardsley. But he also knew that her mind, if
not her heart, was set against his suit, and he did
not dare defy her openly. They met less frequently now, Mary having developed a talent for
eluding him which was most baffling. She seemed
to feel a new interest in all the other young men
and maidens of her acquaintance, and she dis-
tributed her favors with an irritating impartiality.
So persistent was she in this course that a man
less accustomed to having his way, or with less
confidence in the righteousness of his cause, might
well have been discouraged. But Fred Ingraham
had that deeply rooted faith in his own instincts
which a life spent on very close terms with nature,
even in her rougher moods, tends to develop. He
felt that it was not " in the nature of things "—a
favorite expression of his—that such an absolute,
such an unquenchable, such an altogether reasonable love as his for Mary should waken no response. He used to watch her as she moved
about in company, bestowing her frank smile and
quick sympathy upon indifferent people, and in
his inmost heart he said :

"She is mine ! I am the only person on earth
who knows it, but she belongs to me, and there
is no escape for her."

All through those tedious days of wasted
opportunity he never for a moment questioned
his inalienable right in the woman of his choice.

Mary meanwhile did not consciously yield an inch. Any intruding thoughts of this lover, whose very existence was so importunate, she drowned in plans which had a peculiar meaning and fascination for her.

"Summer after next," she would say to herself, "I shall go abroad"; and she marshalled all the wonders and delights of Europe to the support of her resolution.

A needless help had she felt as certain of herself as she thought she did. Surely Mary William was the last girl to marry any man out of tenderness for his feelings. She was not weakly soft-hearted. Other feelings than his must have been involved before her position could be thus endangered. The story of Mary William's reasonings and self-communings during that memorable holiday season would read like a psychological treatise.

The last night of the old year—which was also the last night of her visit at home—was to be celebrated with a "social gathering" at the Rev. Mr. Ingraham's house. Mary was arrayed for the occasion in her claret-colored cashmere, intending to accompany her family to the very stronghold of the enemy, when a sudden misgiving seized her, and she decided not to go.

"You may say I have a headache, if you like," she told her mother.

"But, Mary, it will never do to leave you alone in the house. You know Bridget is going out, and we 've let the furnace fire go down, and you 'll take cold."

"I can light a fire in the hall grate," said Mary. "That will make the house warmer when you come in. Besides, I shall go to bed early."

When the house was quite empty, Mary moved a small table up before the fire, placed a lighted lamp upon it, and armed with an old guide-book of Switzerland, which she had borrowed of one of her cousins, sat down to a cozy evening. Strange to say, the book did not seem interesting, the shadows among the pillars in the dimly-lighted hall disturbed her, and, worst of all, she found herself thinking of Fred. She probably should not see him again for a long time ; there would be no more need of evasions, no more reasonings with herself. She had a feeling that she had passed through a time of probation, and a certain lassitude crept over her which was soothing, after the perplexities and self-discipline of the past ten days. She let her thoughts take their own turn, knowing well where they would tend. It was such a pity about Fred ; he was so much nicer than any one else. Yes, she could afford to say it, now that it was all over—she liked him "best of anybody."

"Oh, dear," she said, half aloud, with a hard, hungry feeling at her heart, "I wish there was n't any such thing as marrying !"

She watched the blue flames dancing on top of the bed of coals, and the little rows of sparks run-

ning along the soot at the back of the chimney—
"folks going to meeting," she had been taught
to call them. Somehow the suggestion of a
string of people all bound for the same place
made her feel cross.

"Everybody's always doing just the same thing
as everybody else. It is so tiresome! If nobody
else had ever got married, Fred would never have
thought of anything so foolish"; and then she
laughed at her own childishness. She would
have liked to cry just as well as to laugh, but she
usually drew the line at tears.

It must have been about nine o'clock when
there was a sharp ring at the door-bell. Mary
shuddered. Was it some midnight marauder?
Alas! her forebodings were worse than that.
Thieves and murderers she might perhaps know
how to deal with, but there was an enemy more to
be dreaded than they. The bell rang a second time,
reverberating loudly through the empty house, before she answered it. Her worst fears were realized.

"Why, Fred, is that you?" she said, holding
the door half open in a gingerly manner. "Did
mother want anything?"

"No. It's I that want something. Are n't
you going to invite me in?"

"Oh, yes! Come in. I was so surprised!
How could you leave your party?"

"That was easy enough. I just walked out of
the room. How pleasant it looks here! This is
the hall you dislike so much. Pity you should!

It makes an uncommonly good setting. And the fire is so pretty! I don't wonder you liked it better than a crowd of people. We burn wood at the ranch—great logs four feet long. They make a blaze to warm the very cockles of your heart. May I get a chair?"

Mary had never known him to be so voluble, but she was not in the least reassured by his flow of words.

"What are you reading?" he asked, as he sat down on the other side of the fireplace.

Her fingers still clasped the red book, though she had not opened it for an hour past. At mention of it, she recovered herself.

"It is Murray's guide-book of Switzerland. Have I never told you that I am going abroad summer after next?"

"Really? How enterprising you are!"

"Oh, it can be easily managed. You know I have quite a princely income."

"Mary," he cried, abruptly, "give up your income, give up Europe, give up all those plans. Come with me! Not now—of course you could n't —but next summer."

She shut her lips firmly together, and stared at the fire.

"See!" he went on. "I put it in the baldest words. I concede everything from the very beginning. I know you would be giving up everything you care for; I know I am asking a perfectly tremendous sacrifice."

"Would you make such a sacrifice for me?" she asked, in a hard, dry tone. "I love my way of life just as well as you do yours. Would you give up your ranch and come and teach school with me?"

"That's not a fair question, Mary. You might as well ask if I would wear girl's clothes to please you. You would n't respect me if I did."

"I don't agree with you at all," she said, sharply and argumentatively. It did not sound like her pleasantly-modulated voice. "I don't see that the sacrifice would be any greater for you than for me. My work and my ambitions are just as necessary to me as yours are to you. And you would never think of sacrificing yours for my sake."

"I 'm not so sure that there is anything under heaven that I would n't do for you, Mary," he cried, impetuously. "But that is something you would never ask. You would n't be yourself if you did. Men sacrifice their lives for women, not their careers. It would not be in the nature of things for you to ask of me what I am asking of you."

He paused a moment, and then he was sorry he had done so. Her face was set and repellant. But she spoke before he could stop her.

"No, Fred, I can't do it," she said; "and please don't talk to me any more. Did n't mother say I had a headache?"

"As though I believed that! I don't believe

you ever had a headache in your life. And supposing you have? What is a headache, I should like to know, compared to a heartache? If I can bear to hear you say no in that horrid cold voice, you can bear to hear me talk as long as ever I choose. Mary, you *shall* hear me, and I am going to tell you something that will make you think you hate me. You know that I love you with all my heart and soul. But it seems foolish to talk about that. Of course I love you. Who could help it? Cousin Letitia adores you, though she may not tell you so. Everybody adores you, simply because you are the most perfectly adorable woman that ever lived. But, Mary," and his voice sank to a lower key—"Mary, there is one thing you don't know, and that I am going to tell you—*you love me.*"

"How *dare* you say such a thing to me, Fred Ingraham?" cried Mary, springing to her feet, white with anger, her eyes flashing, her breath coming fast.

"I suppose it does sound like a brutal thing to say," he admitted, "here in the house, where everything is conventional."

He was also standing now, leaning back in the shadow against the chimney, watching Mary's face with the uncertain firelight on it. The lamp was behind her. She had not got her breath sufficiently to speak again. The red book had dropped to the floor, and her hands were clinched. As he looked at her a sudden pity came over him.

His voice was tender, as though he feared to hurt her more.

"I had meant to walk home with you from our house, and tell you then, Mary. There is lovely starlight outside, and out under the stars one does n't mind the truth. We have wonderful starlight on the ranch, Mary. The air is so clear out there that you almost feel the stars throb. When I have been keeping watch the night after a round-up, riding round and round the great black mass of sleeping cattle on the wide black plains, it has seemed to me as though there were nothing real and lasting in all the universe but just those stars. Now there will be one thing as real and lasting as they, and that is my love for you. And, Mary, you may deny it; you may fight it down and try to kill it, but I tell you solemnly, you will never look at the stars again as long as you live without knowing that you love me."

She had clasped her hands now, and held them tight together, but she would not lift her eyes from the fire. It seemed like a disembodied voice that she was listening to, and there was a strange compelling power in it that frightened her. She made a movement as though she would protest, but he interrupted her.

"Don't, Mary. Don't say it again. Wait till you can say yes. Wait, just as you are, and think. I know you will say yes if you wait a little. You are too true not to see the truth."

Then she lifted her face in the firelight. "Fred Ingraham," she cried, in a despairing tone, "I believe I do hate you—you are—so—cruel."

Fred looked at the tragic face, and an exultant light came into his own.

"It 's a kind of hate I 'm not afraid of, Mary," he said, and he held out his arms.

The shadows among the baronial pillars seemed to be swaying and wavering before her eyes, and her own step faltered. But she went to him, because she could not help it. He kissed her, rather cautiously, and she made no resistance. A strange, delicious, poignant happiness overwhelmed her.

That night Mary cried herself to sleep for the first time since she was a little child. But in that beneficent storm of grief her last tottering defences were swept away. When, but a few hours later, the time of parting came, her valiant lover knew that her surrender was complete.

Mrs. Beardsley generously forgave her young cousin for robbing her of her "treasure," though, as her short period of possession went by, she learned still better to measure her impending loss. She permitted herself but one form of revenge, which, however, she always clung to. As often as she had occasion to write to him in after years, she never failed to address him as her "dear bandit."

As for Old Lady Pratt, though Mary had gone contrary to all her prognostications, she was too much relieved to resent being put in the wrong. Her unfailing comment when the event was discussed in the family was : " Mary William 's got more sense, arter all, than I giv' her credit for."

IX

A VALENTINE.

EVERYBODY liked Mattie and Hattie Pratt, and it would have been strange if such had not been the case. Even the fact of their universal popularity failed to create cavillers. The boys and girls of Dunbridge would as soon have thought of questioning the merits of the sunshine and the west wind, as the claims of Mattie and Hattie to their loyal good-will. Indeed the simile is not inapt. The dark-eyed Mattie, four years the elder, had in her disposition much of the staying, heart-warming quality of sunshine, while there was a refreshing breeziness about her sister which was ever welcome and ever new.

It had been something of a trial to Mrs. Ben Pratt, who was not without a sense of euphony, that the exigencies of family relationship should have obliged her to name her two daughters Martha and Harriet. The inevitableness of the descent to "Mattie" and "Hattie" could not be denied, and the hopeless lack of distinction in the reiteration of that flat *a* was very depressing to a woman who was something of a *connoisseur* in names, having herself been born a Hazeldean. But Ben would not hear of calling the first daughter for any one but his wife, and when, four years later, the second girl appeared upon the scene, Mrs. Ben could do no less than reciprocate, by naming her for her husband's eldest sister, Harriet. More especially since a boy, whose arrival had intervened, bore his mother's maiden name of Hazeldean. By the exercise of great vigilance and determination Mrs. Ben succeeded in keeping Hazeldean's name intact, but this effort so exhausted her energies that she yielded the " Mattie " and " Hattie " almost without a struggle.

Names, however, owe their chief significance to the people who bear them, and it rarely occurred to any one but Mrs. Ben that the names Mattie Pratt and Hattie Pratt could be improved upon.

On second thoughts that statement demands modification. Before the time of our story—when Mattie had reached the mature age of twenty-three—more than one young man had thought that his own surname might be substituted with advantage for hers. Unfortunately for these young men, Mattie had not been of the same mind. She had considered the claims of each candidate with a deliberateness, which in a less sincere and kindly young person might have been censured, and then she had skilfully trans-

formed the misguided aspirant into a more or less
resigned friend.

The nineteen-year old Hattie had, up to this
time, boasted but one actual "offer." It was on
the day that Dickie Lewis first went into trousers,
that he set himself to sue for the very sticky hand
of his young contemporary in a gingham apron.
This interesting scene occurred during the school
recess, the maiden of his choice being at the
moment engaged in eating molasses candy behind
the currant bushes. A large piece of this delecta-
ble concoction was rapidly reducing itself to its
original consistency in her warm little grasp,
while he made his declaration of undying devotion. Little Hattie gazed with the most flattering
interest at Dicky in his newly acquired dignity.
Those trousers were very imposing. But yet, but
yet, she felt in her heart of hearts that she loved
Jimmy Jones, with the court-plaster on his nose,
better than she loved Dicky, and truth compelled
her to say so. Touched by the hopelessness of
Dicky's case, she held out to him the whole big
piece of molasses candy, and to her mingled relief
and chagrin, he seized and devoured it, with
an appetite unimpaired by his disappointment.
Hattie Pratt's faith in manly devotion had never
recovered from that crushing blow. As she grew
older she regarded the comings and goings of her
sister's lovers with a certain scepticism, and when
any rash young man ventured to bestow upon
her a sentimental word or look she remembered

Dicky Lewis and laughed it off. Thus it will be seen how an early disenchantment may eat into the fabric of one's faith in human nature.

Among the frequenters of the Ben Pratt house, a stranger had recently enrolled himself, a stranger whose assiduity in calling once a week did not escape Hattie's mocking criticism. He was the new head-master of the high-school, a tall, grave-looking individual, who wore glasses and limped slightly. Indeed, his limp was so very slight that the irreverent Hattie concluded that his shoes were too tight for him.

Mr. Emerson Swain, for such was his classic name, had seemed so particularly fitted for his post as schoolmaster, and so entirely unfitted to play any lighter rôle, that his arrival in town had occasioned very little comment or inquiry. Nothing was known of him beyond the fact that he had come highly recommended by the authorities of a Western college, that his learning was probably profound, and his social talents correspondingly limited. On the occasion of his first appearance at a social gathering in Dunbridge he had made the acquaintance of the Pratt girls, and, to every one's amusement, it became evident that he had straightway fallen a victim to Mattie's charms. With old-fashioned punctiliousness, he had, a few days later, sought an introduction to Mrs. Ben, and asked permission to call upon herself and her daughters. From that time forward he was a weekly visitor at their house. He usually came on Saturday evening, as a reward, Hattie declared, for having " tried all the week to be good." It was his habit to remain exactly one hour, which time was passed in conversation with Mattie and the elder members of the family. Hattie, who had no mind to allow herself to be shut out in the cold, and who usually sat by with Dixie, the fox-terrier, in her lap, used occasionally to throw in a light-minded observation, thus giving an unexpected turn to the conversation, and causing Mr. Emerson Swain to gaze benignantly at her through his spectacles. " It is such fun to make him blink at me," the bad child would say, when remonstrated with by her family.

Mr. Swain's conversation was quite worth listening to in a very different spirit from that which Hattie deigned to honor it with. Mrs. Ben maintained that he had "the best informed mind " she had ever met with, and she confided to her mother-in-law, Old Lady Pratt, that she almost hoped that Mattie might fancy him.

" It 's high time she fancied somebody ! " the old lady had declared, true as always to her faith in early marriages. Mattie, for her part, listened most politely and attentively to all the schoolmaster had to say, responding in a ladylike manner, which seemed to give him entire satisfaction, if one might judge by the regularity of his visits. She did not acknowledge, even to her family, that she found such elevated conversation a trifle tedious.

14

"Why do you stay in the room when Mr. Swain calls?" she would ask Hattie. "You might just as well be amusing yourself in the library."

"Oh, but he amuses me," Hattie would cry. "He 's just nuts! He arranges his sentences so beautifully, and his spectacles look so owlish. Do you know, Mattie, he seems a great deal too old and solemn to fall in love."

"Very likely he is," assented Mattie, for the two girls had agreed between themselves that he must be "well over thirty." "There is n't any question of his falling in love, as far as I know."

Now Hattie Pratt, though not of a literary turn of mind, had a certain knack with her pen, which had stood her in good stead in more than one of the small crises of her lively existence. One day in February she might have been seen curled up in the cushioned window-seat of the parlor, in close consultation with the lyric muse. It was a Sunday afternoon, and she had some misgivings as to the godliness of her undertaking. But, unfortunately for her Sabbath-day morals, an incident had occurred on the previous evening which had filled her with thoughts of vengeance, whose execution would no longer be deferred.

Mr. Swain had been speaking of one of the assistant teachers at the high-school, the teacher who had the misfortune to stutter as often as he became at all agitated, and Hattie, who was a natural mimic, could not let pass such an opportunity for the display of her powers. At mention of the young man's name, she cried, in excellent imitation of him: "B-b-boys! Such b-b-behavior is inexc-c-cusable."

Their visitor had looked at her reproachfully through his glasses, and had said, with most uncalled-for emphasis: "Yes, Miss Hattie, it is a cruel infirmity."

For once, Hattie's ready wit had deserted her. To her consternation and disgust, she felt the blood rush to her face, and she dropped her eyes before those penetrating spectacles, in unwilling acknowledgment of defeat. She shuddered even now as she thought of her discomfiture, and then she wet the point of her pencil on the tip of her small, unruly tongue, and applied herself with renewed concentration to the work of vengeance. The day had been beautiful. The level rays of the sun, which was sinking in the west, fell aslant of Hattie's curly brown head, revealing a picturesque disorder, which frequent wild clutches for inspiration had wrought. With her feet drawn up under her, and her head bent over her work, all semblance of her graceful little person was lost. Suddenly her brow cleared, her pencil raced over the paper, and, with a sigh of successful accomplishment, she sat up straight, extending her slippered feet to the end of the cushion, leaned her head against the casement, and fell to reading her effusion :

"TO MY CHOSEN SWAIN.

"Kneel not at another's shrine,
Rather come and kneel at mine.
Black eyes cold and cruel be,
Black eyes are not meant for thee.
What my name, and what the hue
Of my eyes, I 'd tell thee true,
But, too timid to confess,
I must leave thy wit to guess,—
Guess the secret that is thine,
If thou wilt be my Valentine."

"There! If that does n't make him blink his conceited old eyes," she thought, with vengeful glee.

The sun was already cut in two by the line of a black hill on the horizon. Hattie turned and looked straight into the golden disk. Her strong young eyes, which had fallen before a certain pair of spectacles, did not waver in the face of the god of day. Her cheeks were flushed from the mental strain of composition, and her eyes were bright. As the sun dropped behind the hill a golden light crept up into the sky, higher and higher, and then the most beautiful waves of color spread themselves along the line of low hills. The young face softened, the lips that had been so firmly compressed relaxed into their natural sweet expression, and a dreamy, far-away look came into the dark-blue eyes. The splendors of the sunset deepened and grew, and then the color faded, and the last uncertain light fell upon the face of a sleeping child, a face where long dark lashes fringed the closed lids, and a mouth as innocent as a baby's was parted in a half smile.

When Hattie awoke, however, at the lighting of the gas, the spirit of mischief awoke with her. For though her face had softened when the sunset color swept the sky, her hard little heart had not changed one bit.

She ran to her own room where she would be safe from disturbance, and there she copied her verses in an elaborately disguised hand. For tomorrow would be St. Valentine's day, and the shot must be fired early in the morning.

Accordingly, when her father was starting, the next day, to drive into the city, she gave him the letter "to post in town." Ben, to whom all girls' scrawls looked exactly alike, did not observe anything peculiar about the handwriting, and readily undertook to do his daughter's bidding. Ben was a fairly obedient father in all small matters, and as such was a great favorite with his children. As the day went by Hattie was full of self-glorification.

"He may not get it till to-morrow," she reflected, "but he will know it was sent to-day, and won't he be puzzled? Oh! I *am* so glad I did it! I am *so* glad I did it!"

Poor Hattie! Her joy was to be short-lived!

"Father, did you post my letter?" she asked, as she helped him off with his great-coat that evening. Mr. Ben Pratt's face was red and his whiskers prickly with the frost as Hattie had discovered when she kissed him a moment before. The dutiful father beamed with inward satisfaction, as he rubbed his hands together to get them warm.

"Better than that! Better than that!" he answered. "I met Mr. Swain just as I turned into Main Street, and for once I had my wits about me."

"You did n't give him the letter!" cried Hattie, in breathless suspense.

"That 's just what I did do," her father answered, complacently. "I told him it was something my daughter Hattie had asked me to post, and I thought perhaps he could find the owner," and Ben passed on into the warm library without a glance at the miserable little victim of his ill-judged zeal.

Hattie meanwhile had fled up-stairs, with pert little Dixie close at her heels. As she shut the chamber door behind her, Dixie, at the risk of his life, dashed in, giving a squeal of anguish as the door nipped his tail.

"O Dixie, you poor little angel," she cried, seizing the small imp in her arms, "did I squeeze his tail in the door? Oh! how could I?" and she tenderly laid him on the bed, and knelt beside him, incoherent and distracted. "O Dixie! Dixie! That horrid man! And your poor little tail! And he knows who wrote it! And he will think !—oh ! what won't he think ! And how it must have hurt, you poor little martyr. And oh, dear, how I wish I was dead ! O Dixie ! Dixie ! did it hurt very bad ? "

All this time the " poor little martyr " was beating the coverlid with his injured tail, and industriously licking his mistress' nose and chin and eyebrows, saying, as plainly as he knew how, that he had forgotten all about his tail, and the best thing she could do would be to forget all about that horrid man too. And then the supper bell rang, and Hattie had to wash away the traces of her tears and go down and face her family, Dixie following close behind. At supper Hattie seemed to be in hilarious spirits, which her family attributed to the half-dozen valentines she had received in the course of the day. She chattered like a magpie, and gave Hazeldean tit for tat in a manner that delighted her father, and caused her mother to wonder whether she would never grow up. But all the while a certain foolish bit of doggerel was ringing in her ears, sending the blood in sudden tingling waves up among the curls in her forehead.

> " Guess the secret that is thine,
> If thou wilt be my Valentine."

Ugh-h—

> " Black eyes are not meant for thee."

Oh ! how hideous it all was ! How perfectly hideous !

The next day went by, and the world had not come to an end. Wednesday came, and Thursday, and Hattie began to wish that something would happen, if only to end this wretched suspense. And then on Friday something did happen.

It had been raining hard all day. The streets were rivers and the side-walks ponds. Hattie had been shut up in the house for so many hours that she suddenly discovered that she could not bear it another minute. She declared her intention of going out for a walk, and, wrapped in a long waterproof cloak, with the hood over her head, she was soon splashing along the sidewalk in her rubber boots, the excitable Dixie racing on ahead and barking wildly. She did not carry an umbrella. Waterproof cloaks had only lately come into fashion, and the owner of one would have scorned an umbrella.

The rain splashed in her face and collected in the "puckers" of her hood. Her hair lay in spirals, beaten flat against her wet forehead. She trudged along, enjoying this conflict with the elements as much as she could enjoy anything just then. She looked at the gambols of Dixie with the melancholy indulgence with which an aged person regards the sports of children. Still that miserable jingle pursued her, echoing through her brain with senseless persistency.

> " Kneel not at another's shrine,
> Rather come and kneel at mine."

Would she ever touch pen to paper again?
No! Never! Never! Never!

She was out on the long bridge now that led to
the city. She did not often get so far as that in
her walks, even on a fair day. Here the wind
had room to rage, unimpeded by trees or buildings. She bent her head and fought her way in
the teeth of the storm, looking neither to the
right nor to the left, where, on either side of the
bridge, the great sheets of ice were being tossed
upon the dark waters.

Suddenly Dixie gave a joyful bark of recognition, and a pair of long legs, clad in much-be-
spattered trousers, appeared a few feet away, in
the line of her down bent vision. She steered off
to the right, but the legs stood still, and an
alarmingly familiar voice exclaimed :

"Why! Miss Hattie! Where are you going?"

"I am going for a walk, Mr. Swain," she said,
distinctly, trying to pass him by.

"For a walk? My child, are you crazy? You
will get blown off the bridge!"

He had turned and was walking by her side.
She said nothing, but pushed on faster and
faster.

"I see you are trying to get away from me,"
he remarked, as he easily kept alongside of her,
in spite of his slightly limping gait.

"I came out to have a walk by myself," she
shouted back, for the wind was roaring.

"I shall not let you walk alone on this

bridge," he declared. His tone of calm authority exasperated her.

"I don't know what right you have to force your company upon me," cried Hattie, lifting her face defiantly, unmindful of the storm that beat upon it.

He looked down upon her, as he walked by her side, and quietly took in the picture. The slender figure battling with the storm, the crimson cheeks and sparkling eyes, the rain-drenched hair, the tiny waterfalls on the end of her nose and chin. The wind suddenly subsided, and it became so quiet that he could hear the splash of the water, as she resolutely tramped along.

"I have the best right in the world to take care of you," he said, in a low, penetrating voice, "because I love you."

"You don't, you know you don't!" cried Hattie, with such vociferous denial that Dixie felt called upon to interfere, and sprang wildly about her and upon her.

The wind had risen again, and her tormentor shouted: "Won't you please turn back now?"

Mechanically she turned, and having the wind at their backs, they went on faster than before. But the bridge seemed to Hattie perfectly interminable. On and on she tramped, with the rain beating upon her shoulders like a hundred hands. Would she never get away from this "dreadful man," keeping pace with her so persistently, and knowing that she knew that he had

said those horrible, those insulting words. For
what was it but an insult to tell her that he
loved her, when she knew it was just because he
had been so stupidly conceited as to think she
was in earnest when she wrote that wretched
valentine.

At last they left the bridge and passed on into
the town, where they were somewhat sheltered
from the storm. They were still two miles from
home. Not a creature was moving in the streets
besides the rain-drenched trio, man and girl and
dog. They might as well have been on a desert
island, for any chances there were of interruption.
And still he walked like a shadow at her side.

"You contradicted me just now," he said at
last, firmly and deliberately, "and so I must
tell you again that I love you. I have loved you
ever since I knew you, but I did not think I
should tell you so. It was not very likely that
you would ever care for a half-blind cripple like
me. But at least I could see you often, and hear
your voice, and know a little of what was passing in your mind, and that was something. I
even fancied that we might get to be friends
some day. But when you sent me that valentine, although, of course, you never meant me to
know who wrote it, I knew it was either one of
two things—either you liked me a little, or you
despised me. And though I am afraid I know
your answer beforehand, I must have it. Hattie,
am I right? Was it one of those two things?"

"You *don't* love me!" she cried again, with increasing vehemence. "You *don't* love me! You love somebody else! You have n't any right to talk to me like that. You thought I meant that odious valentine. I did n't mean it. Nobody meant it. It was nothing at all."

"Hattie," he cried, with a sudden access of anger, which was not altogether unbecoming; "Hattie, you shall not talk to me like that. You *shall* listen to me. You *shall* believe what I say! I do love you—I love you with all my heart. I loved you the first time I ever saw you—I have thought of you from morning till night every day of my life since that day. I love you always—I love you when I am with you, and I love you when you are absent. I love you when you are sweet and kind, and I love you when you are—not sweet and kind. I love all your looks, and all your words—I would dare swear that I love all the thoughts you think!"

On and on they tramped, through the rain and the mud, and on and on he talked. He, who usually " arranged his sentences so beautifully," could not seem to talk fast enough, to say what he had to say. She did not hear half his words. They were drowned and confused by the wind and the rain, by her own bewildering emotions. Only one terrible, overwhelming fact was borne in upon her guilty little soul. He did love her, and she could not help herself.

At last they got to her own gate, and, with his

hand upon it, he said : " Hattie ! Which is it ? Tell me once for all. Do you love me, or do you despise me ? "

Then Hattie lifted up her head and looked him full in the face, and said : "Mr. Swain, *I can't bear you !* "

He opened the gate for her without another word, and, as she and Dixie passed through, he lifted his dripping hat and said good-bye.

Her mother met her at the door, anxious over her long absence, and Hattie threw herself, wet waterproof and all, upon her mother's neck, and cried : "O Mother ! Mother ! He says he loves me ! That dreadful man ! "

" My child, what do you mean ? " cried Mrs. Ben, thinking that Hattie had taken leave of her senses. " Come up to your own room and get off these soaking things."

They went up-stairs, followed by the faithful Dixie.

" He says he loves me, Mother," she lamented again, as her mother pulled off her waterproof, and commanded her to change her shoes and stockings.

" And your petticoats are wet through ! " cried Mrs. Ben. Her motherly heart was in much greater terror of colds than of lovers, which latter dispensation was in the natural order of things, and could not be averted.

It was not until the child was clothed again that her mother was ready to believe that she was also in her right mind, and then she sat down beside her, prepared for confidences.

But, the first rush of feeling being over, Hattie did not find it so easy to tell her story. She looked at Dixie as though she thought he might help her out of the difficulty. But Dixie, who evidently felt that one exciting scene was all that his nerves could bear, had curled himself up in a corner and sought refuge in slumber.

"Well, Hattie, now what is it?"

"Nothing, Mother, only he told me he loved me for more than two miles."

"Hattie Pratt!" cried Mrs. Ben, reduced to extremity. "If you don't tell me who it is that has been talking nonsense to you in all this mud and slosh—*I'll shake you!*"

This, though unquestionably a little mortifying to a young lady who had just received a declaration, was well calculated to recall her to her senses. And Hattie, with the frankness which was one of her brightest virtues, told her mother the whole story from beginning to end, palliating nothing, excusing nothing.

Mrs. Ben heroically suppressed her inclination to smile at this rather comical tale of woe, and, faithful to her sense of duty, said, severely: "And now you have got your deserts."

"O Mother! I did n't deserve anything so bad as that!" Hattie protested. "How can you say I deserved anything so bad as that?"

"Well," rejoined Mrs. Ben, "I think myself

you have been sufficiently punished." She looked for a moment at the woe-begone face of the culprit, and then she said, consolingly: " Hattie, I don't believe he was as serious as he thought for, if that 's any comfort to you. He has probably tried to make himself think he is in love with you, just to spare your feelings. Any *gentleman* would feel bound to do what he could in such a situation,—and Mr. Swain is a gentleman, if he *is* a little stiff in his manners."

" I think, Mother," Hattie replied, with conscious dignity, " that if you had heard him talk, you would not have any doubt about his being in earnest."

Nor did Hattie ever admit any question on that point. Emerson Swain's words, and still more his manner, had been too convincing. She could not mistake the accent of sincerity with which he had said: " I love you." Gradually the first horror with which those words had filled her wore away, and she began to think of them with something very like toleration. It was as though they were repeated over and over every day, so haunting was the tone of voice in which they had been spoken. After all, he was a man, this grave, self-contained schoolmaster. It was a man's love that had been offered her, and not a boyish fancy. There was something wonderfully stirring in his honest passion, which had asserted itself so stoutly, in spite of his self-distrust and genuine humble-mindedness. She could not forget his words—she could not forget him, though she saw no more of him in the weeks that followed. A strange humility had come over her. She began to feel as though an honor had befallen her, of which she had shown herself unworthy. She had not been enough of a woman to accept it, or even to appreciate it ; but if she had been a great deal older and a great deal wiser, she might have taken it differently. She was sorry he did not come to the house any more. His conversation had really been very interesting. She would not have understood anything about the Mexican colonization scheme, and the tragic fate of Maximilian and Carlotta, if it had not been for Mr. Swain. He had promised, too, to take them all over to see the glass-works some day. She would have been glad to see the glass-works. Nobody else would ever think of taking them there. None of the young men they knew seemed to be interested in anything but themselves and their own concerns.

Perhaps Hattie might not have drawn so many comparisons in favor of her lame and spectacled suitor if his society had been thrust upon her. But ever since that eventful walk he had studiously avoided her. The blustering winter months had stormed themselves out, April, with all its sweet caprices, had gone the way of other tears and smiles, and now May had come, bringing young leaves and dandelions, and making green the lawns and hedges. And in all that time Mr. Emerson Swain had only once come to the house.

That was on an evening when he knew perfectly well that Mattie and Hattie had gone to a dance, and he made no pretence of having come to call on any one but their mother. Mrs. Ben had enjoyed his visit very much. She had found him so talkative and easy—not nearly so stiff in his manners as he used to be—that she felt justified in assuring Hattie that if he had ever suffered from any disappointment he must have got over it entirely.

But Hattie knew better. That faith in the immortality of love, which most young girls cherish, had asserted itself in her heart. Emerson Swain, who had given up the game with a half-pitiful, wholly-contemptuous smile at his own expense, would have been surprised and touched if he had suspected anything of the almost passionate loyalty with which his scornful little divinity believed in him.

Meanwhile the last of May had come, and Decoration Day was close at hand. Decoration Day, which meant so much when first it was celebrated, soon after the close of the war. It seemed that year as though the very flowers knew why they bloomed, and pressed forward to meet the day. In the fields about Dunbridge the daisies and buttercups ran riot, and all the brooksides were blue with long-stemmed violets. Brilliant columbines grew about the rocks, and fragile wood anemones and hardy cornel blossoms hid side by side in the woods. All the young people of the town had been out gathering them, and now, in the late afternoon, a score of them were met together in the high-school building, to weave their flowers into wreaths, and sword-hilts, and crosses. The next day the boys and girls would walk in procession, led by the little company of veterans, to lay the fading offerings upon the soldiers' graves. The youngest child who was to carry a posy could remember the war. There was no need to tell him what all these flowery tributes meant.

The group of young people in the schoolhouse worked together, subdued and solemnized by the memories the day recalled, and when the work was done they quietly dispersed, carrying their flowers with them to be kept fresh till morning. On the way home Hattie Pratt remembered that she had left her scissors behind her. She slipped away from the others, and, burdened with flowers as she was, she ran back alone to the schoolhouse. About her neck was a garland of daisies, a wreath of buttercups hung from her wrist, while other wreaths and garlands filled her arms.

Her light step made little sound as she ran up the stairs and into the great hall, the door of which was open. There among the litter of bright blossoms and green leaves stood Emerson Swain,—with his hands behind him looking down. In her haste Hattie had come close upon him before she saw him. She gave a little cry of consternation and started to leave the room. He too looked disconcerted, but when she turned to go he pulled

HATTIE.

himself together and said very composedly, "Don't let me drive you away, Miss Hattie. You have come back for something."

"Only my scissors," she stammered, "but it is n't of the least consequence."

"Let me help you find them."

And he began moving the fallen leaves and petals about with his cane. The scissors soon turned up. As he handed them to her he said :

"You will perhaps be glad to hear—that is, if you care about it one way or the other—that I am going away for good in July. I have not told any one yet, for my new appointment was only settled this morning."

Hattie stood still in helpless embarrassment. She felt that she must say something. She could not go away leaving such an announcement as that in mid-air. It would be too cowardly. At last she gave a constrained little laugh, and asked, inconsequently :

"What do you think of all this clutter in your schoolroom, Mr. Swain ? "

He hesitated a moment—

"Would you like to know what I was thinking when you came in ? I was wondering whether the fellows who got killed did not have the best of it after all. Whether it was not better, for instance, than hobbling through life ? "

"But—but—you were not in the war ? " cried Hattie, suddenly forgetting her embarrassment and self-consciousness.

" And why not ? "

" And did you get——"

" Yes—I got shot."

Her eyes were big with wonder.

" Oh ! please tell me about it. When did it happen ? How did it happen ? "

" It happened early in the war—I got well enough to go back again."

" You went back again after you had got shot ? "

" Of course I did. I was not such a cripple that I could not serve. A lame leg," he added bitterly, " disables a man more in after life than it does in action. Men respect their captain none the less for being a little damaged."

" Oh ! What did they do to thank you ? "

He looked down upon the glowing young face rising up out of the garland of daisies, and he wished she would go home and not stay there looking like that. But he said in a matter-of-fact voice :

" They treated me very well—they made me a colonel before we got through."

" A colonel ! How brave you must have been ! "

And then, as she stood before him and met his eyes, into which a look had come which she did not quite understand, her self-consciousness came rushing back upon her, and she turned abruptly and awkwardly enough and left him.

She went down stairs and out into the long yellow sunlight, thinking new and solemn thoughts.

It was the first time that Hattie had ever been

brought face to face with a personal heroism that rose above the commonplace of every day. It appealed to all her enthusiasm—all her idealism. It touched her as nothing else could have done, it made a woman of her. And yet she was still so much a child that her mood changed from moment to moment, her thoughts flew from great things to small, and all the while she never dreamed whither she was tending.

He had been in the war. He had stood his ground when the bullets whistled about him, when men fell dead on every side. He had been wounded, crippled, and then he had gone back and faced the bullets again. And Hazeldean had dared to call him " a muff." And she ! And she ! Oh ! What had she been thinking of to treat him so ! And she might never see him again. If he had avoided her for three months it was not likely that he would do any differently in the little time remaining. But she must ask his forgiveness. She could not let him go away forever with those contemptuous words to remember. He had offered her the devotion of a brave man, and like a petulant child she had flung back the proffered gift with scorn and contumely.

Then, as a sudden anti-climax, came the memory of certain foolish words she had once spoken. Oh ! dreadful thought ! She had said his shoes were too tight for him ! That smote her conscience more cruelly than all the rest, and without knowing when she had turned, she found herself hurrying back to the schoolhouse, with a wild terror lest he should be gone, and she should have lost her last chance to ask his forgiveness.

She ran up the stairs and burst into the room. There he stood, where she had left him, looking at the flowers that her feet had trodden upon.

"Mr. Swain!" she cried, still panting from her rapid walk, "Mr. Swain, I have come back because I was afraid I should never see you again, and I wanted to ask your pardon."

He looked down upon her, very gravely and indulgently.

"Ask my pardon for not liking me? You could not help it, little girl. There was no reason why you should have liked me. It was kinder to be truthful."

"But I was so rude! Oh, I was so abominable. Won't you please forgive me?"

"Miss Hattie," he said, his voice vibrating in spite of all he could do, "I will tell you something that I hope you may never have to learn in any other way. When a man gets maimed for life he does not particularly care whether it was a gunshot or a swordcut that did it."

"And you won't forgive me?" There were tears in the beseeching childlike eyes, and yet, in the gesture of entreaty, a certain dignity which was more appealing still.

"I don't see anything to forgive," he answered, with a strong effort to govern his voice. "But if it will make you any happier—yes—I forgive you."

He held out a very cold hand, which she took, dropping some of her flowers at his feet.

"I am so sorry!" she said again, pleadingly, with her hand still in his.

"Sorry you do not love me?"

"Sorry I said I did n't," she whispered very, very softly. But Emerson Swain thought he should have heard that whisper if he had been in battle, with the roar of the cannon in his ears.

They walked home together in the long afternoon light, home to Ben and his wife, whom they found pacing the garden path arm in arm. These long-tried lovers looked incredulously at the apparition coming toward them. It was many weeks since they had seen this tall, limping figure within their gates. Did that usually grave face ever before seem so young and animated? did those gray eyes ever before send such a cheerful challenge through the intervening glasses? And more perplexing still was their own Hattie, decked out like a sacrificial lamb, with a look of radiant meekness in her face, which yet was a little pale and awe-struck.

She had not a word to say for herself, but Emerson Swain was under no embarrassment.

"Mrs. Pratt," he said, as they stopped before her, "Hattie has promised to be my Valentine henceforth and forever."

*   *   * . *   *   *

"And I believe they will be very happy," said Mrs. Ben to Mr. Ben, as they talked it over later in the evening. "He is not exactly the kind of man I should have supposed Hattie would fancy, and she is rather scatter-brained to begin life as the wife of a college professor. But they love each other, and that is the principal thing."

"Yes, Martha. That is the principal thing. There 's no doubt about that. I don't suppose it really makes any difference in the end," Ben added, with a chuckle of ill-disguised fatherly pride, "but, as far as I can make out, Hattie seems to have done most of the courting!"

X.

OLD LADY PRATT.

OLD LADY PRATT was failing, and being a shrewd old lady, even at the age of ninety-one, she was very well aware of the fact.

"My faculties ain't what they used to be," she would say, with all her old decision in statement. "I ain't what I used to be, nor what my mother was at my age, and I ain't goin' to be flattered into thinkin' I be."

Everybody liked Old Lady Pratt, though many people were a little afraid of her. Her bright, black eyes dimmed as old age crept upon her, but they rarely softened. The deep, clean-cut furrows in her dark face were the marks of alertness, good-sense, and humor, rather than of gentler qualities. A black "front" with a straight, uncompromising muslin "part," hid the grace and dignity of her white hairs. Her speech was always incisive, often piquant, but never tender. She sat so straight in her chair—thanking Heaven that she had a back of her own—that she never gave that impression of feebleness which makes old age so irresistible in its appeal to the kind-

233

.

hearted. Dr. Baxter, the oracle of the neighbor-hood, used to say of her, that she was "keen as a brier," and that was the accepted estimate. The respect in which she was held among her acquaintances was negatively indicated by the fact that nobody ever thought of calling her little, though her height was, in reality, a trifle short of five feet.

She suffered no pain nor discomfort in her latter days, and she was willing enough to "bide her time," but after her ninetieth birthday she began to realize that life had lost something of its relish.

"Grandma," said her great-grandchild Susie one day, "when you are a hundred years old your name will be in all the papers."

The old lady turned her gleaming spectacles upon the rosy young person of sixteen, and a queer look came into her face. "I hope my name will be in the papers before that," she said, curtly.

"What do you mean, Grandma?"

"Mean, child? Why, among the 'deaths and marriages,' to be sure."

Miss Susie was rather a thoughtful child, and after gazing for a moment at the red flicker in the isinglass window of the stove, she said, "Grandma, would you like to live your life all over again just as it has been?"

"Yes, I should," said Old Lady Pratt. "For one reason," she added in a lower tone.

"I should think it would make you tired to think of all those years."

A wonderfully bright, youthful look came into the aged face. "Nothing could make me tired if your grandfather was alive again. But there! What do you know about that?"

"I wish I could remember Grandpa Pratt," said the little girl, sympathetically. "Tell me about him."

"There is n't much to tell. Only he was the best man that ever lived, I do believe. You 've seen his picter?"

"Oh, yes, Grandma; and it looks so much like Sir Walter Scott's."

"He was a great reader of Scott, and had a very high opinion of his works. But I always said it was just as honorable a calling to be a builder of houses, like your great-grandfather, as to be putting up castles in the air that never kept the rain off anybody's head."

There was a silence, during which the isinglass gave an occasional crackle, and once the whole body of the stove seemed to stretch itself and sigh profoundly.

"Susie," said grandma, after a while, "I hope you ain't goin' to be like your old-maid sisters. There 's Bella, twenty-five years old last 'lection, with no more idea of marryin' than she had ten years ago. Mark my words, child, a woman should be early married. Your grandfather was courtin' me when I was your age, and at seventeen I was a happy bride."

"But, Grandma," said Susie, deprecatingly,

yet with a light-hearted laugh, "there is n't a single person courting me. What am I to do about it?"

To the old lady it was no laughing matter. She frowned a little and looked slightly contemptuous. The rising generation seemed to her very slow and unenterprising, in spite of their railroads and telegraphs. Was a man more a man for being whisked over the earth's surface at the rate of twenty miles an hour? Stuff! How many of them would walk from Framingham to Boston and back, as her grandfather had done, to fetch a betrothal ring for his sweetheart? She wore the ring to-day, a thin gold circlet with the outlines of a coffin just discernible inside. The words, " Till Death " had worn quite away since it came into her possession.

But Old Lady Pratt's mind did not often dwell upon the rising generation and its shortcomings. Even the great-great-grandson, in whose small person the family beheld its fifth generation among the living, had but a transient hold upon her attention. From him her thoughts wandered to her own grandchildren and their pranks, and there were certain reminiscences, especially of Uncle James, the eldest, which the children were never tired of hearing.

" Grandma," they would ask, " how did that spot come on the ceiling?"

Now there was in reality no spot whatever on the ceiling. It had had many a coat of whitewash in the last forty years, whose passage had left so little impression on the failing memory.

"That spot!" Grandma would answer. "I can't seem to see it very plain, but I guess that must be the spot your Uncle James made when he was a little boy."

"Why, how could he make a spot so high up?"

"He threw a spit-ball."

"Why, Grandma! And what did you do to him?"

"Do? I *boxed him!*"

This always came out with a snap, which delighted the souls of the children.

"You did, Grandma? Poor Uncle James!"

"Poor Uncle James, indeed! He was as impudent a young rascal as ever lived."

"Why, what did he do?"

"He looked up in my face and said, '*You Paddy!*'"

Nothing could be better than grandma's relish of this story. She was not a great talker, however. In fact, her daily life was a peculiarly silent one, her only companion being her unmarried daughter, Betsy, whose deafness precluded all possibility of conversation. There had been a time when the old lady fretted a good deal about this.

"It does seem to me," she would say, "as though Betsy's deafness would drive me crazy." Or again, when very much vexed : "I do believe it ain't all deafness. The girl has n't got any spunk, that's the trouble. If she had, she'd make out to understand something now and then by her wits."

But this had been when grandma was only seventy or eighty years old, and the impatience of youth was not yet wholly subdued.

Now it was different. She had got used to seeing the large, loosely built figure always at her side, with its slightly bobbing head, which had once been such an annoyance to her, and she had come to appreciate the unobtrusive virtues of a faithful slave.

Aunt Betsy had not much spunk, it is true. Her wits seldom came to the assistance of her imperfect faculties. But she knew all her mother's needs and wishes by heart; and the absolutely unswerving devotion, day by day, and hour by hour, of the sixty odd years of her life had come, by the mere process of accumulation, to have the weight and importance in the old lady's mind which they deserved. The black eyes of the elder woman often looked approvingly at the meek old face in its pretty frame of soft gray curls. It was a pity that Betsy never knew that the reason she had not been allowed the dignity of a "false front," to which she had so ardently aspired, was because her mother thought her curls "too pretty to be covered up."

Once in a great while when Betsy had rendered her some especially timely service, the old lady had called her to her side to say: "Betsy you're a good girl. I don't know what I should do without you." And Betsy had gone about with a warm feeling at her heart for weeks after.

Thanksgiving had always been a great day in the Pratt family, for then its scattered members came from far and near to keep the good old festival. Their numbers had years before outgrown the capacity of the little old house in Green Street, and the celebration had been transferred to "Harriet's."

Harriet was Mrs. Pratt's eldest daughter, the widow of a rich man, and she dwelt in a very grand house, with a terraced lawn in front and a cupola atop, a house where any family might be proud to meet together. Her long, wide parlors, with their thick Turkey carpets and their red velvet furniture ; the large mirrors over the two black mantelpieces which were adorned with gilt candelabra hung with rainbow prisms ; the pier glasses at either end, multiplying indefinitely every object in the room ; the numerous oil-paintings which had the air of having been bought by the dozen ;—all this was very splendid indeed.

And the queen of this palace on Thanksgiving Day was Grandma Pratt. Every one paid his respects first to her as she sat bolt-upright in the stiff, high-backed "Governor Winthrop" armchair. Aunt Harriet took but a secondary place in her own house on that day.

It was as queen of the New England feast that the old lady's memory always lived in the minds of her descendants, perhaps because she was more "herself" on the last Thanksgiving of her life than at any time later.

The great dinner with its many courses may have seemed a little long to her, though she drank her annual glass of sherry with the old relish; but it was when they all gathered for a frolic in the brightly lighted parlors that she seemed most thoroughly in her element.

She joined in the quieter games, such as "Button, button," and "Neighbor, neighbor," and grew much excited over the traditional "Blindman's Buff," which she witnessed from a remote corner of the room, Aunt Betsy sitting by to ward off the impetuous "Blind Man" when he made too wild a dash in their direction.

When the young people were tired of romping —they were all young people to Old Lady Pratt— they gathered about in a far-reaching circle, and clamored for grandma's stories of their fathers and grandfathers, and of her own youth.

It was a pretty sight : the wide circle of faces, —old and young, dark and fair, all focusing upon one point—upon that small, upright figure which time had failed to bend; upon those clear-cut, animated features which ninety years had not subdued. It was a picture which the children, old and young, never forgot, and no Sibyl of ancient days was ever listened to with more rapt attention than Old Lady Pratt.

Last of all came the dance, which was the

crowning pleasure of the gala-day. As the circle of her listeners dispersed, Uncle James came up to Grandma Pratt, and with old-time gallantry invited her to lead the Virginia reel with him. After coquetting a little, as she always did, and reminding him that she was an old woman, she suffered herself to be led to the end of the room, and, as the long lines were forming, her little old feet tapped the floor impatiently, and her eyes grew bright behind her gold-bowed spectacles. Mary Anne, who was generally conceded to be the "unselfish" member of the family, went to the Chickering grand piano, and struck up the jolly old jig, not too fast (as it is often played nowadays), but allowing time for the "steps."

Grandma moved lightly forward, and made the preliminary courtesy to her opposite grandson in a manner which should have been a lesson to a degenerate age. She had no more admiring spectator than Aunt Betsy, who could not dance herself, because it made her head swim, and who watched her mother with a sort of awe as she wound in and out in the mazes of the figure, her step brisk, her head erect, and cap-strings flying. Then came the march, grandma leading her half of the procession with great spirit, a light flush coming on her old face, her eyes shining brighter and blacker than ever, while the merry train of revellers clapped their palms together and gayly shouted. Then they all joined hands and formed a continuous arch the whole length of the long

16

room, and Old Lady Pratt, with her favorite grandson at her side, passed down between her children and her children's children for the last time.

She panted a little when they reached the foot of the row, and James said, "I don't know how you feel, Grandma, but I 'm kind o' tuckered out. Let 's go and look on."

"That 's a fib, James Spencer," she answered, sharply. "You think I 'm tired and need to rest."

"You, Grandma? You never get tired. We all know that. But it 's because you 're so light on your feet. I guess you would be tired, though, if you 'd gained fifteen pounds in a year, as I have."

And he escorted her resolutely to the straight-backed arm-chair, which she was glad enough to take, since she had not been obliged to "give in."

It was but a week after this Thanksgiving Day, on which she had seemed so young and gay, that Old Lady Pratt gave Aunt Betsy a great fright by not getting up to breakfast. It was an event without a precedent, and the fact that she only owned to feeling a little "rheumaticky" did not reassure her anxious daughter.

Immediately after the untasted breakfast, Eliza was despatched to summon Harriet, and Harriet was soon at her mother's bedside.

She found the old lady seeming very well and bright, and quite scorning the idea of calling in

Dr. Baxter. Rheumatism, if rheumatism it was, was an entirely new guest in the sound old frame, and Harriet did not quite believe in it.

Just as she was about to leave her mother she said, abruptly: "Have you done anything to strain yourself, Mother? It don't seem quite natural for you to give out all at once so. Come, tell me."

The old lady looked up at her from among her feather pillows and said, rather petulantly: "You always was a sight smarter 'n Betsy. I sometimes think you 're a leetle too smart."

Harriet sat down again, not ill pleased to be thus taxed with an excess of smartness.

"Tell me about it, Mother."

"That 's jest as I choose," said the old lady, with some defiance in her tone. "Will you promise not to tell anybody?"

"Of course I will if you say so. Did you fall on the ice?"

"Not exactly."

Then, with a curious manner, half-reluctant, half-amused, she said: "I went out into the kitchen yesterday afternoon when Eliza was up attic changin' her gown, and there was that curtain over the sink all askew ag'in. I 've spoke to that girl about it forty times if I have once, and I was too mad to speak the forty-fust time. So I thought I 'd fix it myself and it might be a lesson to her."

"But, Mother, you could n't reach it! You 're not tall enough."

"A pretty state of things it would be if we could n't get hold of anything that was out of our reach!" the old lady retorted, with ready paradox. But she did not seem to want to go on.

"Well, what did you do?"

"Do? What would anybody do? I got a chair and climbed up on the edge of the sink."

"Dear me! And did you strain yourself?"

"No. I had a fall. But I fixed that curtain fust; straighter 'n it had been fer some time."

"And you fell onto the floor, all that distance? I don't wonder you feel lame."

"Well, no"—and here the reluctance became more evident,—"I fell *into the sink!*"

She looked defiantly at her daughter, as though daring her to laugh. This the daughter had no inclination to do.

"But, Mother, how did you ever get out?" she asked anxiously.

"Oh, I got out easy enough. But I felt kind o' stiff this mornin'," she admitted, after a pause, "and I thought I 'd see how you 'd all take it if I was to lay abed for once in my life. But mind you don't let on to anybody," she added, more sharply. "I ain't goin' to be the laughin'-stock of the neighborhood in my declinin' years."

The old lady was about again in a day or two, but she was pretty lame after this, and, indeed, she never seemed quite the same again. She would sometimes fall asleep in her chair—a thing which she had never been known to do before—and she was always mortified and vexed when she awoke.

One afternoon she started up suddenly from a nap, saying, "Betsy, what did you say?"

"What is it, Mother?" said Betsy, turning her head to listen.

"What did you *say?*" asked the old lady.

"Nothin', Mother, nothin'."

The strained voice became a little querulous. "Betsy, I ask you what was you a-talkin' about?"

"Nothin', Mother, nothin' at all."

Then a flash of anger, her last fit of "temper," lit up the old eyes, and she cried, "What was you *a-thinkin'* of?"

"Nothin', Mother, nothin'," declared the bewildered Betsy.

"Betsy, I *heard ye!*" screamed the baffled old lady; and she sank back exhausted, only to fall asleep again in a few minutes.

Yes, Old Lady Pratt was breaking up. She did not "take to her bed," as the saying is. She died one morning before "sun-up."

For a few days before her death she kept her own room, sitting, still upright, in the stuffed chair, in her sunny south window. It was January, and the snow lay glittering on the ground.

"I like it; it 's so bright and cheerful," she declared, when they asked her if it was not too dazzling.

Betsy did not leave her side for several days and nights, till at last Harriet insisted upon taking her place for what proved to be the last night.

She arrived, escorted by one of her grandsons, early in the evening, and they went directly up the narrow stairs. As they reached the upper landing they heard a strange sound—an aged, quavering voice crooning a lullaby.

The door of the bedroom stood open, and a candle was burning dimly. The old lady sat in her stuffed chair, with her faithful daughter close beside her. She held one of Betsy's hands, which she stroked softly from time to time, as she sang, in a high, broken treble, to the old tune of "Greenville":

> "Hush, my child; lie still and slumber;
>   Holy angels guard thy sleep."

Betsy, alas! could not hear the familiar lullaby, but she felt the caressing touch. The gray head nodded gently, as was its wont; but the passive look upon the patient face, across which the light of the candle flickered, had given place to one of deep content.

Harriet and the boy turned and crept down the stairs again, the boy hushed and embarrassed, Harriet crying softly to herself.

"I'm glad I came," she said, with a sob—"I'm glad I came. I think mother'll die to-night."

Old Lady Pratt "passed away" very quietly. The going out of the light which had burned so bravely and steadily for more than ninety years was almost imperceptible to the watchers at her side.

The next two days were for Betsy a time of bewilderment. She sat, with a dazed look upon her face, receiving the visits of condolence. As one neighbor after another entered and pressed her hand in respectful sympathy, she would rouse herself to say, in a vague, wandering voice: "Mother's gone. Yes, mother's gone." And then she would sink back into silence, while the conversation went on about her in subdued tones.

"Poor Aunt Betsy!" they all said. "She's quite broken. It almost seems as though she were losing her mind."

Ah, it was not her mind she was losing, poor soul! She could have better spared that. It was the heart which had quite gone out of her.

Happily she was saved any acute feeling of sorrow in those first days by the merciful apathy that had fallen upon her. She was like a boat that has slipped its moorings, but floats upon a quiet sea. There were no wild tossings to and fro, no great waves to swallow up the fragile bark. It might drift far out on the darkening waters, or the incoming tide might rudely crush it on the rocks. For the moment it floated gently and aimlessly upon the bosom of the deep.

The stir and excitement of the funeral roused Betsy somewhat. She was pleased with the wreaths and crosses and other floral emblems which were sent in, making the air of the little house heavy with their fragrance. She was even interested in her own mourning when they brought it to her and helped her put it on. Each token of respect, each ceremony of grief, gratified her, as a tribute to the imperious little woman who had ruled her every thought and action.

There was consolation, too, in the peaceful figure in the rosewood coffin. The face she loved looked so life-like and so serene, that she could not grasp the idea that it must be put away from her sight, that all this pageant, as it seemed to her simple mind, was to end in utter blackness and emptiness.

She was taken in the first carriage with Sister Harriet; and even when the mournful procession slowly moved on its solemn way she was upheld by a grateful consciousness of the long line of carriages, with their many inmates, paying honorable tribute to her mother's memory.

It was a bitterly cold day, and the services at the grave were short—short, but terribly real and final. As she stood there in the cruel wind, poor drifting soul, the inevitable tide was rising, and the rocks were very near.

Harriet was to stay with her that night; and when they had had their dinner and set the house in order, she proposed to Betsy that they should both go to their rooms and lie down.

Betsy had been looking on with a feeling of jealousy foreign to her gentle nature, as Harriet worked with her about the little rooms, straightening the furniture and replacing the ornaments upon the tables. She was thankful to be left, for a time, at least, in possession of her own, so she meekly went up stairs and lay down on the bed, while Harriet retired to the " best chamber."

The rocks were very, very near, and the poor soul was fast drifting upon them. She lay upon her bed for a few minutes in helpless misery. Then she got up, and sat awhile in her window. The mere inaction, to which she was unaccustomed, was distressing to her, but she did not know where to turn for escape.

" Oh, dear ! " she moaned softly to herself; " oh, dear ! I ain't got anybody to do for any more."

She got up and went into her mother's room, and moved about, taking up and putting down again the little personal belongings : the faded pin-cushion on the bureau, the old receipt-book, the worn spectacle-case with the steel-bowed glasses,—the gold spectacles had only been worn on " occasions," and were kept under lock-and-key. She went to the great double-bed with the calico flounce around it, and softly smoothed the pillows.

By and by she took a dust-cloth and went over every bit of the furniture. It comforted her, for the moment, when she found a speck of dust to be removed. But when the humble task was finished, the comfort was past.

"Oh, dear! I wish I could do something for her," she whispered, as she crept down the narrow stairs to the sitting-room.

Eliza was making a cheerful clatter in the kitchen, and some English sparrows were squabbling in the snow; but for Betsy's ears there was nothing to break the sense of utter emptiness and desolation.

"Oh, dear!" she kept saying to herself—"oh, dear!"

She moved toward the parlor, where her mother had lain in state. As she opened the door a fierce chill struck her, and she went and got her little gray knit shawl, which she pulled tightly about her shoulders. Everything in the parlor was in its accustomed place, yet nothing was the same. She moved to the table in the middle of the room, and laid her hand upon its hard, cold surface. In the shadow beneath a window she saw a small object lying. She picked it up. It was a little bunch of pansies which one of the great-grandchildren had brought "to Grandma Pratt."

"Oh, dear!" murmured Betsy. "It's the pansies. They've been forgotten. And they was always her favorite flower."

She lifted them to her face a moment, and then she laid them down on the table. By and by she went to the kitchen and fetched a tumbler of water, and set the pansies in it.

After that she wandered aimlessly about again.

"Mother 'd say I was uneasy as a fish," she suddenly said to herself, and sat resolutely down. Her eyes lingered regretfully upon the pansies in the tumbler, and the words, "Mother 'd ought to have them ! Mother 'd ought to have them !" dwelt like a refrain upon her lips. Suddenly an inspiration came to her that made her heart beat quicker. Why should not her mother have them ? She looked out of the window. The sun was still bright upon the glittering snow, though the short winter's day was drawing to a close. "'T ain't so very far," she said to herself. "There 'll be plenty o' time to git back before supper, and Harriet 'pears to be asleep. I do want to do somethin' for mother to-night, and she 'd ought to have them flowers."

With trembling haste she went up stairs to her room, creeping stealthily past the door of the "best chamber." Harriet was sound asleep, as Betsy might have known if she could have heard the heavy breathing within the room. She put on her warmest cloak, which happened to be a black one, and her new black bonnet and gloves, and hurried softly down the stairs. In her haste she had forgotten the "Sontag," which she always wore in very cold weather, and it had not seemed quite decorous to wind her big white "cloud" around the mourning bonnet.

The air struck cold upon her as she closed the front door behind her, and she hid the pansies in the folds of her cloak to keep them warm. "It seems to me colder 'n it did this morning," she said, with a shiver, not noticing that the sunlight was all but gone from the chimneys and tree-tops; "but mother 'd ought to have them pansies; her favorite flower, too!" Her teeth chattered as she hurried along, stumbling now and then, but there was the warmth of an eager purpose within her. "I wanted to do somethin' for mother; I did want to do some little thing for mother." The dusk was gathering fast about her, but she knew the way. "I hope they won't miss me before I git back," she whispered, with a guilty look at the darkening sky; "they might git worried." And she pushed on, faster and faster, through side streets and alleys, an increasing eagerness urging her on as she approached her goal.

Harriet's family and Anson's had lots in the new "Woodland Cemetery," but Old Lady Pratt and her husband were lying side by side in the quieter resting-place of their own generation, known as "the old burying-ground."

There was no wind stirring, and as Aunt Betsy hurried on and on, and saw the stars coming out in the clear sky, there was a growing gladness in her heart, and she scarcely noted the deadly chill that was creeping upon her.

The gates of the old burying-ground were never locked, and there was nought to hinder her as she pushed them aside with her benumbed hands and entered in.

The Pratt lot was in a sheltered corner not far

from the entrance, and Betsy went to it, without hesitation. There it was, with its row of modest head-stones, and the black break in the snow, which marked the newly made grave. It looked very black indeed in the starlight, and Betsy shuddered with a feeling stronger than the outer cold.

She laid the pansies, wilted with frost, upon the dark mound, and then she sat down on a bench in the shelter of the high board fence to rest. The sky was sparkling with stars, and she looked up at them with a sudden glow of hope and joy.

"Mother's up there," she said within herself, for her cold lips refused their office. "Seems to me as though I could see her eyes a-shinin' down. I wonder if she's pleased to have them pansies?"

A feeling of warmth and well-being stole upon her as she sat on the old bench, gazing no longer at the dark grave, but at the starry heavens.

Yes, it did seem as though her mother's eyes were shining somewhere among those stars, and as she looked longingly toward them there sounded in her poor unhearing ears the sweetest words that had ever reached them: "Betsy, you're a good girl; I don't know what I should do without you."

Over and over, like a sweet refrain, those words sounded, while the sense of warmth and brightness deepened upon her. Then her eyes closed but did not seem to shut out the glory of the heavens. And hearing still those comforting words, her gray head dropped upon her breast, and she fell gently and happily asleep.

After a night of anxious search, they found her there in the early dawn.

"Poor Aunt Betsy!" some one said. "She must have gone crazy."

"That ain't the face of a crazy woman," said Brother Ben, with a choke in his voice. "It's the face of a transfigured saint. God bless her!" And he knew in his loving heart that already the benediction rested upon her.

MARY ANNE.

"THANK you, dear child."

The voice in which these words were spoken was of that soft, uncertain quality in which a hint of querulousness may be detected. The speaker's face was the face of a nervous invalid.

"Thank you, dear child," she said sweetly, and her daughter's cheeks flushed with pleasure. Mary Anne Spencer knew no greater joy than a word of appreciation from those lips could bestow. She left the room with heightened color and elastic step.

"How unselfish Mary Anne is!" said Mrs. Spencer, as the door closed behind her daughter.

The remark fell upon unheeding ears. Mr. James Spencer was far too much engrossed in his evening paper to give a thought to so commonplace a theme as Mary Anne's unselfishness. Every one knew that Mary Anne was unselfish, every one said that she was. There was no more doubt on the subject than upon the color of her hair or of her eyes, and those who praised her were totally unconscious of the patronizing tone which lurked in their commendations.

Unselfishness is a virtue which is seldom questioned, but, if carried to excess, it places its owner at a manifest disadvantage. It is a hindrance to personal success, and whoever may have first made the statement, the world surely did not wait for his utterance before discovering that " nothing succeeds like success."

James Spencer, himself a successful man, unacquainted with the first principles of self-abnegation, did not concern himself ·much with his daughter's character. She was useful to him in many ways, but her personality failed to interest him. He would not have acknowledged even to himself that he found her amiability monotonous. Indeed, Mary Anne's " crying virtue" as her father once called it in a moment of irritation, had never awakened a distinct misgiving in any one's mind, excepting in that of her father's grandmother, Old Lady Pratt.

" Don't talk to me about Mary Anne's unselfishness!" the independent old lady would exclaim. " I 've no patience with her."

" But, Grandma!" would be the rejoinder, " don't you think her spirit of self-sacrifice is very beautiful ?"

" A fig for her sperrit of self-sacrifice ! Before you know it, it 'll be all the sperrit she 's got left ! I can tell you something that 's a long sight better than self-sacrifice, and that 's a good, wholesome bit of self-assertion ! We wa' n't made to lie down for other folks to walk over. What 's the good of a backbone, I should like to know, if not so's we can stand up straight and make the most of the chances the Lord gives us ! ''

This had been the old lady's stand from the very first, and she held her position stoutly to the last. The '' unselfish '' Mary Anne had always given her greater cause for uneasiness than did Mary Anne's scapegrace brother Tom, who, in his boyhood, was the despair of his other elders.

One day, in her extreme old age, Old Lady Pratt gave still stronger expression to her views than she had hitherto done. For on this occasion she took her daughter Harriet (Mary Anne's grandmother) into her confidence on a point which she had never before touched upon.

'' I tell you what 't is, Harriet,'' she said, with her old eyes snapping, and her knitting-needles glinting faster than ever. '' I tell you what 't is ! I ain't lived ninety years in this world without findin' out that a little *spunk* is as good for other folks as 't is for yourself. It 's my opinion that women like Mary Anne do more mischief than they 'd relish bein' called to account for. There 's Betsy, now ! You don't 'spose I 'm any the better for havin' ordered her about for more 'n sixty years runnin' ? ''

The old lady looked at her patient daughter with a softened, pitiful expression.

'' Poor Betsy ! She ain't to blame, seein' she 's deaf as a post. She 's a good girl, and she 'd ben smart 's anybody if she could only ha' heard a

17

little of what folks was sayin'. But there! There's no need o' cryin' over spilt milk. All I've got to say is, there ain't no sech excuse for Mary Anne, and I declare for 't, I sometimes feel 's though I should like to *shake her.*"

Now neither the many who praised, nor yet the one who censured, really had the clue to the girl's character. Old Lady Pratt, with all her shrewdness, supposed, as the rest of the world did, that Mary Anne was inherently and spontaneously unselfish. That when she gave up pleasures that others might enjoy them, when she sacrificed her own inclinations that she might do a service for some one else, it was because of a quality in her nature different from anything in her companions.

The truth was, however, that Mary Anne's unselfishness was a refuge, to which she instinctively had resort, impelled thereto by her two ruling characteristics—self-distrust and a craving for approbation.

Mary Anne was the eldest child of James Spencer, a man of peremptory manners, though of a really yielding disposition. His other children had never found any difficulty in "getting round Father." It was only his eldest daughter who stood in awe of him. This may have been one reason why she was not a favorite with her father. From the time when she was a little child, his commands and admonitions had frightened her. He had a way of coming to the foot

MARY ANNE.

of the stairs, when there was too much noise in the nursery, and saying "Hst!" and that sharp, penetrating sound would send cold shivers down her back, even when she was doing her best to keep her little flock in order.

She was very young when she began to regard the little ones as her special charge. Her mother, who had little of what our grandmothers called "constitution," had always had her own hands full with the care of the youngest baby, and she had left the others more and more to Mary Anne's guidance and oversight. Mary Anne appeared to take naturally to the task. To all the world she seemed to be a good, plodding girl, quite without desires and aspirations on her own account. The fact that it took brains as well as patience to accomplish what she had always done never seemed to dawn upon those about her. All her usefulness, and no one denied its magnitude, was attributed to her being "so unselfish," and, proud of the one virtue with which she was credited, Mary Anne clung to her reputation and, unconsciously perhaps, endeavored to augment it. So great was her thirst for praise that a word of thanks, a smile of appreciation, filled her cup of happiness to the brim, and no price was too high to pay for such a reward. It must be recorded, however, that none of Mary Anne's beneficiaries were lavish in their gratitude. Her father, as has been seen, took her good deeds for granted and wasted no words upon them. His wife, on her part, had so early formed the habit of shifting the burden of her cares upon her strong young daughter's shoulders, that now, when there were no more babies to tend, she still looked upon Mary Anne as her chief support, and accepted the girl's services as naturally and unthinkingly as she did those of the old family horse, or of the paid house-maids. It was because her "Thank you, dear child!" was rare that it sent the color into her daughter's cheeks.

Mrs. James Spencer's children—and there were nine of them—were a plump and hearty race, and all of them, excepting Mary Anne, were governed by that healthy spirit of self-seeking to which the world in reality owes so much.

"Mary Anne! Mary Anne!" was the cry from morning till night. "Mary Anne! Come and help me do my sums!" Or: "Mary Anne! I 've torn a streak-o'-lightning hole in my trousers!" Or: "Mary Anne! I 've made a list of errands for you if you 're going to town." Sometimes a careless "Thank you" was tossed her for these services; oftener, perhaps, it was forgotten.

If any one of the children was taken sick in the night Mary Anne was sure to be called up, and young Dr. Winship, who had succeeded to his father's practice, declared that she was a "born nurse." If Miss Plimpton, the dressmaker, was employed by the day it was Mary Anne who settled down, quite as a matter of course, to do seamstress work until the dressmaking dispensa-

tion was past. It was Mary Anne who played
backgammon with her father of an evening ; it
was Mary Anne who bathed her mother's head
when it ached ; who beguiled the younger children
to bed with tales of gnomes and fairies, of good
little girls and bad little boys ; it was "Miss
Mary Anne" to whom the servants came in any
domestic emergency. She used sometimes to
wish that she had been given a gentler, more
musical name, since she was to hear it called in
so many keys, by so many voices, to so many
ends. She had been named for her mother, who,
however, had always been called "Nannie."
"And she 's always been treated 'Nannie,'"
Mary Anne sometimes said to herself, rejoicing in
the gentleness with which everybody approached
the delicate, dependent woman. Mary Anne
loved her mother with a devotion which was
maternal in its tenderness and generosity ; and
next to her mother she loved her troublesome
brother, Tom.

Tom, the "scapegrace" of the family, was
four years her junior. He was no less bent upon
having his own way than were his brothers and
sisters. But where they simply demanded, he
wheedled. Now wheedling involves many little
expressions of affection, with a pinch of flattery
thrown in, and now and then a kiss crops out in
the process. When Tom told Mary Anne that
she was the best sister a fellow ever had he was
merely making a statement of fact, which the

others, if called upon, would have willingly
endorsed, but it so happened that he was the only
one who ever thought of putting his opinion into
words. And when he had made some such
demonstration, Mary Anne's cheeks would flush,
and all day long she would gloat over the recollection as a miser gloats over his gold. She was
not as unconscious as so good a girl should have
been. When she played the piano for a whole
evening that a party of boys and girls might
dance, she was not above reflecting that they
owed their enjoyment to her. When she had
stroked her mother's temples until her arm felt
like anguished lead, and when she finally saw
sleep steal over the worn face, she would glory in
the thought that it was she who had brought
relief. She would have begrudged the office to
any other hand. Happily, Mary Anne was not
morbidly conscientious or introspective. Had
she been so, she would have detected her own
foibles, and all her innocent pleasure would have
been spoiled. She was now twenty-six years of
age, and she had never yet thought of living a
life of her own. There was only one very strong
desire which she cherished on her own account,
and that one desire was for a musical education.
She had been taught piano-playing when she was
a little girl, but after she had attained such pro-
ficiency as to be able to play for dancing, the
lessons had been stopped. She had a strong
musical bent, and practising was still her one

indulgence. She played Beethoven sonatas and Mendelssohn Songs Without Words, in her own way, which was a much better way than any one had yet discovered. Her mother's mother had recently died, leaving each of her grandchildren a legacy of five hundred dollars, and Mary Anne intended using it for music lessons whenever she should "get time." The money, meanwhile, had been placed in the savings bank, where it might increase itself to this excellent end.

But one day Tom came begging, and before he left her she had loaned him her $500, for a secret purpose which he could not reveal, but which he was "sure she would approve." Tom was in a banker's office, and had doubtless heard of a promising investment, and nothing could have seemed more natural than that he should have the use of her money.

One fine evening in April Mary Anne found herself mistress of the house and of her own time. Her father had taken his wife and two of his daughters to hear Christine Nilsson sing. The two youngest children were in bed, and the rest of the family were scattered in one or another direction. The evening was mild and the house rather warm. Mary Anne opened the parlor windows, lighted the candles in the brackets of the old square piano, and fell to practising the *Moonlight Sonata.* Untutored as she was, there was nothing ordinary or slipshod in the girl's playing. What she lacked in technique was more than atoned for, to the uncritical ear, by the spirit and expression with which she played. She had practised long and carefully on this sonata, and to-night, for the first time, she was giving rein to her fingers. She played the third movement, with its splendid crescendos and beautiful periods, three times over, each time with gathering impetuosity and passion. It was something to arrest any listener.

So at least thought one passer-by, as he paused at the gate. It was young Dr. Winship, a man of German tastes and traditions, to whom the *Moonlight Sonata* was an article of faith.

"Who on earth can that be?" he asked himself.

The young man had a great liking and respect for the family in the large, rambling yellow house, with the little white fence around the roof, and the pear-trees in the front yard. He liked them all very much, and he flattered himself that he knew them pretty thoroughly, but he had never discovered any musical genius among them.

Mary Anne was just beginning the movement for the third time, and the opening passages went rolling up and on like great ocean breakers. Dr. Winship listened a few minutes with growing incredulity, and then he opened the gate and walked up the path. Just as the performer, rather breathless and excited, had finished the move-ment he was ushered into the parlor. There sat his "born nurse," in the soft, transfiguring candle-light, turning a starlit face toward him, and rising with a dazed, uncertain gesture to meet him.

But she was herself in a moment, and came forward, saying deprecatingly :

"Oh Dr. Winship ! I am so sorry everybody is out ! "

"It did n't sound as though everybody were out a moment ago," he said, grasping her hand very warmly. "I came in to thank you for your music."

"Did you like it ? " she cried, with a childlike spontaneous delight which was very winning.

"Does n't everybody ? " he asked.

"I never play to anybody except for dancing."

"I hope you will play for me sometimes. But not to-night." he added, gently. "You have played yourself into a fever."

It was the most delicious thing Mary Anne had experienced in all her life. First the praise and then this solicitude and gentleness.

"Where did you learn to play ? " he asked presently, as he sat beside the music-stand looking over the little collection of pieces.

"I never learned. That is just the trouble," she said. "I took lessons till I was twelve years old, and then it got crowded out."

"Crowded out, when you were twelve years old ! What a busy child you must have been ! "

She laughed and said, " I 'm afraid I was only slow."

" Are all your people out to-night ? I was in luck !—I mean," he corrected himself, " I was in luck that you should not have gone too."

" They have all gone to town to hear Nilsson."

" I wonder how they managed to leave the musician of the family at home." The situation made him unconventional.

" Father could only get four tickets," she answered simply.

Dr. Winship suddenly remembered that he had always associated this girl with household cares, that he had found her on three separate occasions established as night-nurse in a sick-room, that when he had called socially, he had invariably been told that Mary Anne was " playing back-gammon with Father " or was " up-stairs with Mother." A feeling of indignation got the better of him.

" Miss Spencer," he asked, " do you never by any chance have any good times ? "

Mary Anne gave her questioner a surprised look. Then she replied with a sort of apologetic dignity :

" I always have a good time."

" Is that so ? Then you are the first person I ever knew who got her exact deserts."

Having thus relieved his mind, the visitor discreetly left personalities alone. They fell to talking of music and of Germany, of foreign peo-ple and remote things, and for one reason or another, both these young people became entirely absorbed in conversation, and both felt a pang of regret as the tall clock in the dining-room sent its solemn voice echoing through the house proclaiming the hour of ten.

Dr. Winship sprang promptly to his feet, for he prided himself upon knowing how to go. But before precipitating himself out of the door, as was his wont, he shook his entertainer cordially by the hand, and said, with unmistakable sincerity: "I don't know when I have enjoyed an evening so much. May I bring my violin next time?"

"Next time!" The words sounded like music, the very clang of the closing door resounded like a pæan through the house.

As Mary Anne stood in the middle of the room, trying to get her balance, there was a sharp rap on the door which she opened hastily.

"Have you seen the new moon over your left shoulder?" asked the young doctor, with amusing eagerness. "It has rained so much lately I thought you might have missed it."

"No. I have n't seen it. But you ought to look at it over your right shoulder."

"Oh, no! That 's a great mistake. The Germans, who are up in mystic lore, taught me better."

She held back doubtfully.

"I 've always been so particular about it," she said.

"Well, now. Just trust to me, and try it the

other way. See, it will be gone behind the church in a few minutes. There! stand that way and turn your head to the left. There now! See if you don't begin to have good luck as is good luck."

She laughed a delighted little laugh that was pleasant to hear.

" I always supposed you were all science," she cried.

"And I always thought you were all useful-ness," he retorted. "It is a great relief to know the truth about you."

" And I'm very glad you're so light-minded."

She had her hand on the door to go in. Her face, turned toward the moonlight, looked won-derfully youthful and sweet. Mary Anne's cares had after all been of a kind to leave the spirit unclouded.

" Did you ever breathe anything so good as this air?" the young man asked, actually linger-ing on the brink, as he had seen and despised others for doing.

" It's the spring," she answered, simply. He remembered her attitude and the tone of her voice, years after, when they listened together to the same words set to heavenly music.

" Miss Spencer," he cried; impulsively, " I wish the next time anybody is sick, you would let somebody else sit up with them. It would do them good."

She shook her head with much decision.

"There is n't anybody else—and, besides, I like it."

"There 's the usefulness cropping out again," he cried. "Good-bye."

"And were n't you a trifle professional just now?" she called gayly after him.

Then she closed the door behind her, and stood in the brightly lighted hall, trying once more to get her bearings.

How foolish she was to be so excited and happy over a little thing. It was probably just like what was happening to other girls all the time. She had had a very pleasant evening, of course, but what of that? And there were the candles on the piano burnt down to their very sockets, and she must go directly and make a cup of tea against her mother's return.

She busied herself with this and other duties, and tried to bring herself to reason, but do what she would, think what she would, she was changed, and the next morning before breakfast she determined not to put off any longer getting herself a spring suit, even if the rest of the family were not already provided for. This, in itself, was enough to prove that a revolution had taken place in her mind. Yet so strongly did her old life-long habits assert themselves as the day wore on, that, but for an opportune catastrophe, she might again have fallen a victim to them.

The second day following her pleasant evening was a New England holiday, the 19th of April.

Mr. Spencer did not go to his office in town, and Mary Anne was not surprised to be summoned to him in the library. She went, prepared to render some chance service, or answer some question about household affairs. To her consternation she found Tom there, looking very pale and desperate, standing before his father, whose face was stern and lowering.

"Well, Mary Anne!" was her father's greeting. "Here's a pretty state of things!"

"Why, Father. What's the matter?"

"Matter enough! Tom's been gambling in stocks, and owes a thousand dollars, and there's nobody to blame for it but you."

"Father!" Tom remonstrated.

"Hold your tongue, Tom," cried his father, hotly. "It's exactly as I say. If Mary Anne had n't been an absolute fool, she would have known better than to lend you money. I don't count that among his debts," James Spencer added, bitterly. "It serves you right to lose it, and I, for one, shall not make it up to you."

"But, Father," Tom began again.

"Hold your tongue, Tom. Do you hear me? Tom's been a fool, too," he went on, turning to his daughter; "but he has at least had the manliness to own up. He's not quite lost to all sense of decency yet. But he's headed straight down hill. He's got a taste for gambling, and if he goes straight to the deuce, I swear there's nobody to blame but you."

Mary Anne stood half stunned by the violence of the attack. Could it be she whom her father was saying such things about? She? She who would have given her life for Tom? She who had never had a thought for herself? Who had sacrificed every natural wish and taste to serve her family? Who had relinquished her little treasure because Tom had persuaded her that it would make a man of him to have a taste of enterprise? *She* was to be Tom's ruin? A hot flush of indignation went over her. For the first time in her life she experienced a great throb of self-assertion. In a voice as peremptory as James Spencer's own she demanded : "Are you talking about *me*, Father? Do you say that *I* have ruined Tom ?"

"Yes, I do ! You have systematically spoiled him all his life ; and now——"

"I have systematically spoiled you all!" cried Mary Anne, with a sudden, uncontrollable energy of rebellion. "Every one of you ! From you, Father," looking him unflinchingly in the eye, "down to little Ben and Jimmy. I 've spoiled you so that you——"

"Highty ! tighty ! Is this the self-sacrificing Mary Anne, who prides herself——"

Again she interrupted him. She was no more afraid of her father now, than she was of the *Moonlight Sonata,* and flinging herself with the whole force of her nature upon the catastrophe, she cried, "I will never be self-sacrificing

again as long as I live ! I will never do another
thing for anybody else ! I am going to be a perfect pig ! ''

James Spencer stared for a few seconds in
speechless astonishment at his daughter, standing before him with flaming cheeks and defiant
eyes. Had she lost her mind, or had she become
possessed of the devil? At any rate she looked
surprisingly handsome, and that at least was as
it should be. A sudden revulsion of feeling went
over him, and holding out both hands to her, he
cried :

'' Mary Anne, come here ! You 're a trump !
I 'm proud of you ! '' He held her hands for a
moment and gazed up at her from his big easy
chair with a look wherein approbation still con-
tended with amazement, and then he said : '' See
that you stick it out, my girl ! see that you stick
it out ! ''

For the moment Tom's misdemeanors were forgotten, and somehow they never assumed the same
gigantic proportions in the family councils again.
In his joy at having his daughter's virtues miti-
gated, James Spencer could afford to be indulgent
to the sins of his son.

When, that same evening, a caller was announced, namely, Dr. Charles Winship, Mary
Anne, with a queer little laugh, said to her younger
sister : '' Edith, I think you 'd better play back-
gammon with Father this evening. I want to
see Dr. Winship myself.''

Then James Spencer openly gloried in the situation.

"Well, Edith," he said, with a comical shrug of his broad shoulders, as he settled himself for his game; "Mary Anne's carrying things with a high hand. You and I may as well submit."

18

XII

WELL MATCHED.

PEOPLE often said of Mr. Richard Spencer and his youngest son, Dick, that they were " well matched." It is to be feared that the comparison was not altogether flattering to either of them, since it was called forth less by the rather inconspicuous virtues which they had in common, than by their more striking characteristics of an irascible temper and considerable stubbornness.

Yet there was something in what wise Old Lady Pratt, Mr. Spencer's grandmother, had said when young Mrs. Spencer confided to her her anxieties early in her son Dick's career.

" Lizzie," Grandma said, " do you recollect our old Topsy, that was always a-layin' in that stuffed cheer when you and Richard used to drop in so unconscious-like of a Saturday evening, and be all struck of a heap to see each other? Betsy, she 'd never believe you was a-courtin'. Old maids are most gen'rally kind o' hard to convince. But my spectacles are pretty sharp ones."

To such sallies Lizzie never failed to respond

with a becoming blush. She was a woman who did not outgrow her feelings.

" Well," Grandma went on, " Topsy was about as fierce a cat as ever lived. I declare for 't, I do believe the critter 'd rather fight than eat any day. But there was one cat he was friends with, and that was Miss Gibbs's Jericho. Jericho he was a master-hand at fightin' too, and it 's more 'n likely that them two tabbies had had one good pitched battle to begin with. But whether or no, there 'peared to be a kind o' bond o' union betwixt 'em. They 'd sit nose to nose on that board fence sunnin' themselves by the hour. Sometimes they 'd blink at each other and wave their tails about kind o' gentle an' innocent. Then agin' they 'd go off to sleep jest as confidin' 's a pair of turtle-doves. Now you mark my words, Lizzie; it 'll be jest so with Dick and his father. They 're too well matched to fight often. They may have it out once or twice before they come to reason, and I don 't say 'tain't goin' to be pretty lively for you. But there 'll never be any small naggin' and domineerin' betwixt 'em, and when once they 're settled down friends, it 'll take a good deal to set 'em onto each other."

Old Lady Pratt was right about this as she was about most things, and before she went to her rest she had the satisfaction of seeing her grandson and his young epitome living as comfortably together as Topsy and Jericho in the sun.

As Dick grew up it was really delightful to see

what good friends the two were. Mrs. Spencer could forgive her husband for falling into an occasional rage with the other children, because he seldom molested her "fire-brand" Dick ; and as for Dick he might "blow out" at her with impunity, so long as he did not rouse the lion which slumbered in the bosom of her chosen lord. She would often watch them as they strolled down the garden path together, thinking the while of Topsy and Jericho and of her early alarms, and she would say to herself with a deep sigh of content, "It has really been a great deliverance."

A sensible woman was Mrs. Richard Spencer, and her husband only hoped that his sons might have his luck when their courting days came round.

The courting days were nearer at hand than Mr. Richard Spencer suspected. Perhaps he had forgotten that he began his own courting at the early age of twenty. Such a lapse of memory could alone account for his not attaching more significance than he did to a little incident which occurred one pleasant June morning when Dick was barely turned twenty-one. The family were assembled at the breakfast-table, grace had been said, and as Mr. Spencer lifted his eyes he beheld an unusual sight. The dining-room windows looked out upon the gravel space in front of the barn. Although it was at some distance from the house, the view was unobstructed, and a top-buggy which had been backed out from the carriage-house was plainly visible. This was a sight to which Mr. Spencer was well accustomed, and there was nothing unusual in the pailfuls of water which were being energetically flung upon the four wheels of the vehicle. It was on this spot and at this hour that the carriages were frequently washed.

But Mr. Spencer's eyesight was good, and he saw, not only the buggy top glistening in the brilliant morning sunshine, and the figure of his trusted servant vigorously swashing the wheels, but in the shadow of the buggy top an object suspended, which bore a striking resemblance to a woman's bonnet. It was of white straw with bright pink roses upon it, and as it hung from the hook provided for the reins, it was lightly wafted to and fro by a gentle morning breeze. It gave Mr. Spencer rather a singular feeling, for the buggy was Dick's, and he looked often from the unique picture before his eyes to the unconscious face of his son. He was quite determined, however, not to make any allusion to the matter, and was rather taken aback when he found himself saying, as he passed his cup for more coffee, " Did you have a pleasant drive yesterday, Dick ? "

" Yes, sir," said Dick, " very pleasant."

" Where did you go ? "

" I went round by Darbon Centre. There are lots of wild roses out," he added, with an air of dwelling upon the point of chief interest.

" H'm ! Did you go alone ? "

" No ; I took a friend."

Dick's manner as he said this was so need-
lessly innocent that his father's wise resolution
vanished, and before he could stop himself, he
had said :

" H'm ! He left his *bonnet* behind him."

Dick followed the direction of his father's eyes,
and looked out of the window. He flushed crimson. There was a shout from John and a titter
from the girls, and Dick, pushing back his chair,
rushed from the table, and seizing his hat, dashed
out to the barn. There they could see him be-
rating the indiscreet groom, who vainly tried to
conceal his enjoyment of the situation.

Poor Dick ! It was no laughing matter to him.
He sternly ordered the man to "let that buggy
alone and harness Golddust." He backed the
horse into the shafts himself, made fast the straps,
and in five minutes after his hasty exit, his
family beheld him driving out of the yard, the
wheels of the buggy still dripping wet, and the
bonnet waving like a banner from the top. A
more defiant and indignant heart never beat
under any flag.

Once fairly out of sight of the dining-room
windows, Dick took the bonnet from its unworthy position and laid it reverently upon the
seat beside him, first spreading his snowy pocket-
handkerchief beneath it. Then he covered it
over with the light lap-robe.

He was a curious study at that moment, in the

mingled fury and tenderness of his aspect. With one hand he clinched the reins, as though seeking to control a wild beast, as indeed he was, though the wild beast's name was not Golddust ; while the other hand rested protectingly on the fragile object beside him. He lifted the cover once or twice and looked at the fanciful combination of straw, ribbons, and muslin flowers. It seemed to his untutored mind a thing of perfect beauty, and its nearness was very soothing to his wounded sensibilities. He reflected that the Mortons were not as early risers as his own family, and not wishing to arrive on his somewhat surprising errand at Julie's house until her people were likely to be dispersed, he turned the obedient Golddust toward the open country. Poor Golddust was much perplexed and hurt by the grim clutch of his master's hand upon the reins. He had a tender mouth and a tender conscience, and he knew he deserved better treatment. But he trotted lightly along the smooth road, and when, after a mile or two, the inconsiderate grip was relaxed, he turned his head a little and laid back one ear in grateful and forgiving recognition of relief.

At first Dick's reflections were very bitter. He felt himself betrayed and wronged in his tenderest feelings. Yet those feelings of tenderness were so much stronger than his indignation about them could be that he gradually gave himself up to them.

It had been his first drive with Julie, and after all nothing could rob him of it now. The lovely June weather, the long, lingering twilight, and the young hearts happy in an unexpressed communion, all had been in tune, while Golddust, with his shining sorrel coat, had seemed like a good fairy, graciously condescending to serve them.

It was at this point in Dick's meditations that Golddust felt the reins relaxed.

The bonnets of that day were heavy, oppressive structures, and Julie had felt the weight and irksomeness of hers. So she doffed the awkward thing as they were driving home through the open country, and laid it in the hood of the buggy, where Dick made it fast to the hook. When the bonnet was gone a hundred little sunny curls were released, and the evening zephyrs played among them in a manner that enchanted Dick.

As they drove into the town half an hour later the stars were coming out, and the hush of a summer evening was in the shadowy streets. The two young people were silent and preoccupied, and when they drew up before Mr. Morton's gate, Julie gave a little regretful sigh, at which a sudden throb of courage inspired Dick.

He handed her from the buggy without speaking, but just as she turned to leave him he seized her hand and cried, in a voice more eloquent than the words :

"O Julie! I should like to drive with you forever!"

Was it any wonder that they forgot the bonnet? That Julie ran up to her little room, her heart beating so hard that she could hardly breathe? That Dick's strong hand trembled as he drove Golddust home and "put him up"?

In the presence of such memories even the Spencer temper could not long rage, and by the time he reached the spot where they had discovered the wild roses, Dick's mind was sufficiently disengaged to receive a happy suggestion. He would fill the bonnet with roses!

In an instant he was out of the buggy, searching for the fairest buds and blossoms, with a heart as light as though it had never stormed. He smiled gleefully as he laid the flowers in their singular basket. It was "made to hold flowers," he said to himself, thinking, with a gleam of fancy, of the flower-like face he had often seen within it. Yes, the boy was too happy to be angry long.

Dick's courtship ought to have been a prosperous one, for he and Julie had loved one another long before they were conscious of it. Furthermore, she was the very maiden whom his parents would have had him choose; and even worldly circumstance, so prone to frown upon lovers, was all in their favor.

But there was an obstacle upon this flowery path which Dick scorned to evade—an obstacle which he had determined to remove, by brute force, if need be, before he would take another step. The boy was totally dependent upon his father, and he was resolved never to ask Julie to be his wife until he was in a fair way to earn a living.

Mr. Spencer was the rich man of the pretty suburban town where he lived. He had made money in the iron business when that branch of commerce was most flourishing, and had retired from active life before the precipitous decline in the iron interest which had wrecked so many fortunes.

He was now comfortably occupied with the care of various trust properties. He was a bank director and president of the local horse-railway, and he held other offices of dignity and responsibility which were gratifying to his pride.

He was not himself a college-bred man, yet he had a comfortable sense of equality in his intercourse with those of his fellow-townsmen who had enjoyed the advantage of a fleeting familiarity with the dead languages, and he had left his sons free to accept or reject such advantages, as they should prefer.

Ben, the eldest, had graduated with honors, and " gone in " for law ; John was established in business in the city, whither he repaired daily in the pursuit of fortune ; while Dick, after a year's trial at college, had fallen into an impatience of books, and announced himself ready for practical life.

Now despite the shrewdness and capacity which had made a successful man of Mr. Richard Spencer, there was an unaccountable streak of dilatoriness in him. He acquiesced in Dick's decision with secret satisfaction. He had always had a peculiar pride in the boy's resemblance to himself, and he was glad to find that he was no bookworm. Yet he could not seem to rouse himself, as he ought to have done, to find a proper business opening for the lad. For nearly a year Dick had been fretting under the delay, for he was an ambitious young fellow, and had no mind to "fool away his best years," as he expressed it. Now, at last, things had come to a crisis, and spurred on by the hope of Julie's love, he was ready to demand a career at the point of the bayonet.

Armed, then, with all the righteousness of his cause, Dick went to the city, a few days after his memorable drive, and confronted his father in his business office. He found him engaged in the perusal of a documentary-looking paper, from which he only glanced up as his son entered to say :

" Hullo, Dick ! What can I do for you ? "

" I will wait until you are at leisure, sir," said Dick. " I 've come to talk business."

" Oh, ho ! " said his father, amused by the importance of the boy's tone. " It 's business is it ? All right ! Business before pleasure," and he folded up an elaborate scheme for the extension of one of the principal railroads in the country at the cost of several millions of dollars, and gravely waited for Dick to proceed. Dick, in his self-absorption, quite missed the point of the little joke.

"Father," he said, with much emphasis, "I 've come to have a serious talk about my future. I 've come to ask you, once for all, to give me a start in life."

Mr. Spencer looked annoyed. "My dear Dick," he said, "this is n't the place to discuss family matters. And besides," he added, rather lamely, "you know very well that I am on the look-out for you. I shall be as pleased as you when anything turns up."

"Things don't turn up of themselves," Dick answered, stubbornly ; "and if you don't mean to lend a hand, I intend to look out for myself."

Mr. Spencer felt thoroughly uncomfortable. It was very irritating to have the "young rascal" take such a tone with him. Yet, as a sort of sop to conscience, he determined to be magnanimous. So he said, not too crossly :

"I don't see what you 're in such a hurry about, Dick. You 've got plenty of time before you. You can't force these things. Come now," he added, persuasively, "why can't you make up your mind·to go abroad with the Wheelers as they want you to, and see a little of the world before you buckle down to hard work ? "

Clearly Mr. Richard Spencer had forgotten about that bonnet.

But Dick was not to be bought off, and he answered : " Because I would n't give a fig to go abroad. I 'm tired to death of shilly-shallying. I say, Father," he added, beseechingly, " there 's nothing I would n't do. I 'd take any kind of a clerkship. I 'd sell goods behind a counter. I 'd go into a railroad office. Can't you get me a chance at the D. & I. P. ?"

" Nonsense, Dick ! It 's out of the question."

" But why ?"

" Why? Good gracious, Dick, can't you see through a ladder ? A salary is n't what you 're after. You don't need the money. And besides, you can't pick up a salaried place at every street corner."

" *I* can't. But *you* could, Father."

This eagerness was a little tiresome, and Mr. Spencer began to look bored. He unrolled the paper which had been subordinated to "business," and seemed to expect his visitor to go. So Dick got up.

" Well, I see you want to get rid of me," he said. There was no answer, and a dangerous look came into the boy's eyes as he added : " I give you fair warning, sir, that as you won't help me, I shall do my best to help myself."

" That 's all right, Dick. Go ahead," his father answered, glad to see the last of him on any terms, and as Dick closed the door behind him, not too gently, Mr. Spencer returned to the consideration of the documentary paper. For some reason he found it less interesting than before. Dick was gone, but the eager, frustrated look in the lad's eyes haunted him.

"I only hope the young rascal won't be playing me any trick," he said to himself. "First thing we know, he 'll be clearing out altogether, and we shall hear of him digging gold among the roughs in California. Confound these youngsters! They all think Rome was built in a day."

Between his disapproving conscience and his fears of some sort of a catastrophe, Mr. Spencer was far from easy in his mind, and he determined to bestir himself in the matter before he was a week older.

But Dick was yet more prompt in action, and before either of them was a week older he had taken measures which were destined to disturb his father's equanimity pretty seriously.

When Dick left his father's office, it was early in the afternoon, and the out-going horse-cars were but sparsely occupied. He stepped upon the rear platform of one, and lighted a cigar for solace and inspiration. He was angry and discouraged. He felt thoroughly defeated. Yet there was a certain satisfaction in having declared open war, and being ready to take the world on its own terms. In the course of his recent boyhood, Dick had scraped acquaintance with most of the employés on this old-established road, and he soon fell into conversation with the conductor. Preoccupied as he was with the great subject of bread-winning, he got his companion to talk of his work and of his pay, and the rich man's son felt honestly envious of the independent possessor of such work and such wages.

"Do you know, Bill, you 're a mighty lucky fellow," he said. "*I 'm* such a beggar, I can't get a chance to earn a nickel."

The conductor looked at him in some surprise. Then he said, jocosely : " You might come on the road. I 'm going to try and get transferred onto the new Leanton branch. It goes nearer my folks. I reckon I could get you my place." And the honest fellow grinned with pleasure in his own humor.

"By Jove !" Dick cried : "I guess we 've struck it this time ! If that would n't fetch the governor, nothing would."

The old woman with the bandbox who came out of the car just then, and the young woman reading a library book at the farther end of the seat, little guessed that a dark conspiracy was going on before their very eyes. But when Dick swung off the step, he called out : " I 'll see you to-morrow, Bill," and walked toward Julie's house with the tread of a conquering hero.

The conspiracy ripened fast ; so fast that in less than a fortnight after that momentous conversation on the rear platform Dick emerged from the company's office an accepted candidate for Bill Geddings's place. The superintendent had "liked his looks," had pronounced himself satisfied with

Bill's voucher, and had promptly enrolled the singularly familiar name of " Richard Spencer " on the list of conductors.

It was with mixed feelings that the new conductor walked from the office. He had applied for the position in a reckless mood, and was surprised to find himself rather elated with his success. Quite apart from his frankly acknowledged hope of coercing his father, it was really very gratifying to know that an impartial judge seemed to consider him " worth his salt."

On the other hand, he was obliged to own that the immediate consequences of this startling proceeding of his might be disagreeable, and it was not without misgivings that he contemplated breaking the news to his father.

" It will be an all-round botheration for the dear old chap," he said to himself with some compunction ; " I hope I can let him down easy."

His plan was to appear before the " dear old chap " after his first day's service, and state his case with as much moderation as he could command. His own position was clear. He proposed to work in the company's service until something better turned up, and he had sufficient confidence in his own often tested obstinacy to know that nothing was likely to shake his determination. Whether the effect on the " dear old chap's " mind would be to hasten or to retard the consummation of his hopes was another question.

Julie, at least, was all encouragement. She

considered his new venture a stroke of genius. She longed to see Dick in his brass buttons handling the bell-punch with all the style he was sure to put into anything he did. She secretly believed that he could have turned a hand-organ with distinction and success.

Julie did not confess all this to Dick, but her confidence was very cheering; and when he entered upon his new duties one morning at six o'clock, he felt as though he were wearing her colors.

Now Mr. Richard Spencer was in the habit of driving to town every day in his own buggy; but it so chanced that on this particular morning he patronized the horse-car. That in itself was a coincidence, but it would seem as though some mischievous kobold must have guided the steps of the unsuspecting old gentleman to cause him to board his son's car. However that may be, this strange and untoward thing did happen.

Dick had stated the night before that he should have an early breakfast, as he was going off for the day with another fellow, and his trusting family had enjoyed their morning repast untroubled by any suspicion that that "other fellow" might be a brawny son of Erin employed as driver on the horse-railroad.

Mr. Spencer's conscience meanwhile had been effectually quieted, and his passing fears of a revolt on Dick's part were consequently allayed. Having once seriously resolved to bestir himself.

he was not the man to waste time, and he had been, for a week past, in correspondence with one of his friends, a manufacturer, who was in search of a junior partner with a fair capital, and sufficient pluck and perseverance to go through with the necessary apprenticeship in the business. The chance was exactly suited to Dick's capacity, and, reflecting upon the pleasant surprise he had in store for the lad, Mr. Spencer walked to the horse-car with a light step and a light heart. As he reached the corner of the street he was gratified to see a car just at hand, and he stepped upon the platform before it had come to a full stop, with an ease and agility which a younger man, and one of lighter weight, might have envied.

A bank director and railway magnate does not often vouchsafe a glance at a street-car conductor, and even the tremendous noise with which Dick was aware that his heart was thumping among his ribs failed to attract the passenger's attention as he brushed past the conductor and entered the car.

Dick promptly summoned his wits and gave the signal to start; but as he stood looking through the glass door at the silk hat, just visible over the morning paper behind which his father was hidden, he devoutly hoped that he might escape recognition.

The car gradually filled up, and the time arrived for taking the fares. Dick grasped his bell-punch and passed from one to the other of the passengers, collecting fares and manfully snapping the spring upon each ticket. He glanced furtively at that silk hat, and wondered that its wearer did not look up startled by the shrill tone of the bell, which sounded to his own ears like the crack of doom. But no one, not even the pale, nervous-looking women sprinkled along the seats, seemed to receive the slightest shock from the "infernal racket" the thing made. At last Dick arrived in front of the silk hat and the newspaper, and a cowardly wish possessed him to pass them by, since their owner seemed oblivious to the situation. But it is one thing to have cowardly wishes and quite another thing to be a coward, and Dick promptly said, as he was bound to do, "Fares, please."

Mr. Richard Spencer mechanically put his thumb and forefinger into his vest pocket, glancing up as he did so at the conductor with the familiar voice. For a moment the passenger seemed turned to stone, while he gazed into the eyes beneath the conductor's cap, his newspaper slipping from his grasp, his fingers arrested in the act of pulling out a ticket.

Then the blood rushed to his face, and he said sternly, though in an undertone, "Quit your tomfoolery, Dick, and leave the conductor's business alone."

" I can't very well do that, sir, as I 'm the conductor," Dick answered, respectfully, while his heart hammered his ribs. His father looked at him, at his cap and his badge, at his bell-punch. Here, then, was the trick he had feared, the defiance he had dreaded. Mr. Richard Spencer was no aristocrat, but this was carrying a joke a little too far.

" Get out of my sight," he growled, between his set teeth. His eyes looked ominous.

" When you 've paid your fare, sir."

" I don't propose to pay my fare."

Dick's blood tingled.

" I 'm sorry, sir," he said, steadily, " but you 'll have to."

Thus far the talk had been low, and not every one could hear what was said. But there was no one in the car who did not perceive that something unusual was going forward.

A man behind him pulled the conductor's coat, and said, in a friendly growl, "Go it easy, young chap ; that 's the president of the road."

" I know it," Dick said, over his shoulder, in grateful recognition of a kind turn. But he stood like a rock before his contumacious passenger.

Mr. Spencer had put the paper up before his face, but the lines went scalloping across the page, and in his consuming anger he took a grim pleasure in knowing that the object of it stood there defying him. It was fuel to the fire, and when once Mr. Richard Spencer's passion was roused he gave himself over to it with a fierce satisfaction.

Outwardly Dick had kept his self-control. He

had a pride in his new calling and a determination to do his duty with propriety and temperateness. But there was a tempest within him which was a match for the passion of the elder man. He spoke very quietly.

"My instructions, sir, are to carry no passenger over this road without the payment of a fare. I hope you will not force me to extreme measures."

At this crisis there was a touch on the conductor's shoulder, and a ticket was thrust before him. "Here, take that," a voice whispered, "and don't rile the old chap any more."

"Thanks," said Dick, as he punched the ticket and dropped it into his pocket. To his ears the bell had a triumphant clang.

The old man had not seen the ticket. "You give it up, do you?" he said, with a sneer, as Dick moved on to the next passenger.

Dick's eyes flashed.

"Your fare has been paid, sir, by one of the other gentlemen."

Then Mr. Spencer, rose, towering in his wrath, and pulled the strap with a vehemence that endangered the stout leather.

"The other gentleman is a *meddlesome idiot*, and you—you—*you* are a *blundering impostor!*" And with this double anathema, the president of the Dunbridge Horse Railway stepped off the car, and stood in the dust of the street, cooling his cheeks, but not the inward fires, in the pleasant breeze that blew about him.

Poor Dick ! The sight of his father standing there, abandoned and exposed, would have been too much for him, had not the old man's last words—"blundering impostor"—stung him to renewed resentment.

As he turned to continue his duties, a general murmur of conversation arose. He caught snatches which made him miserably uncomfortable.

"What ailed the old crank anyhow?" said one voice.

"I reckon he 'd been out on a bat," another chuckled.

"The young feller stood to his guns like a man," declared a third.

At last Dick escaped onto the rear platform, where a shrewd-faced Yankee was leaning against the brake, contemplatively chewing tobacco.

As Dick appeared, he looked up inquiringly, and pointing his thumb over his shoulder, drawled :

"He war n't tipsy naow, was he?"

Dick flared up. "Tipsy ! If I was off duty, I 'd fight the whole car-load of idiots. There 's not one of them that 's fit to black that man's boots."

The Yankee gave the tobacco quid a twist with his tongue, and seemed to be making a study of Dick's heated countenance.

"Waal, I snum," he said, drawling more than

ever. "You 're nigh about as peppery as the old one."

Then, with a slow dawning of intelligence, he added, "I reckon you two have *met before.*"

It had been a disastrous beginning to the day, yet Dick was surprised to find how soon the painful impression wore off. There was an unreality about the whole situation which made it seem like a dream or a bit of fiction. He could not thoroughly believe in his own part in it, and yet there was just a sufficient sense of identity to give zest to the little drama. He found himself in a new attitude toward the great public. The absurd inquiries, which must become so tiresome to an old hand, had for him the charm of novelty. The old ladies, with their unaccountable agitation and their hesitating steps, called out all his chivalry. The toddling children found in him a ready friend and helper, as they vaguely lifted their chubby feet in the general direction of the lower step. When his own acquaintances appeared from time to time, the interest became still more lively. Ladies greeted him with undisguised astonishment, while the men joined him on the platform, and did not hesitate to " pump " him vigorously. Before night the town was all agog on the subject. Every one knew that Dick Spencer was conductor on the horse-railroad, and every one chuckled over the situation, and wondered how the "president" liked it.

By noon Dick's spirits had risen so high that

he was once very near getting himself into trouble.

It happened that a stout, pompous woman motioned him to stop the car at a street corner just as he had his hands full of change, and he was a little late in pulling the strap. The driver was also a little slow with the brake, and the portly passenger gazed with kindling indignation at the gradually receding vision of her garden gate. When at last the car had come to a full stop, she arose in her majesty and approached the door. Arrived on the platform she turned to Dick, and said severely :

"Conductor, why did n't you stop the car at *my corner ?*"

This was too much for Dick's discretion. With an air of elaborate apology, he said : "I beg your pardon, madam ; I did n't know you *had* a corner."

Then, as she flashed upon him a malignant look, he added, meekly, "I will be more careful another time."

The good woman's wrath was tempered with perplexity, and by the time Dick had gallantly assisted her from the platform, there was that in her countenance which told him that he was forgiven. The danger was averted for that time, but the incident gave Dick an entirely new feeling of self-distrust, and he resolved to cultivate the virtue of stolidity.

As the day passed, and he became a little

accustomed to the amusing masquerade, Dick's mood grew more serious. Recollections of his father's discomfiture would intrude themselves upon him. He could not pass the spot, where he had last seen the old man standing in the dust, without a feeling of strong compunction, and he fairly hated himself when he thought of the rôle which had been so unexpectedly forced upon him. He was pondering these things in a rather dismal frame of mind as he stood on the rear platform of his almost empty car, early in the evening of the same day. The exhilaration of novelty was past, and he found himself brought face to face with certain distasteful facts.

He knew his father's temper (and perhaps his own) too well to hope for a speedy reconciliation, and he was obliged to admit that the prospect of an indefinite term of service on the horse-railroad was not altogether pleasing to contemplate. In vain he told himself that it was independence, and that independence was all he had desired. The irrevocableness of the situation — and young people are ever ready with the word "irrevocable"—taught him that what he had taken for independence was nothing but a respectable servitude.

It was still broad daylight. He stood with his back planted against the end of the car, and his hands in his pockets, gazing gloomily at the receding city. The road was deserted; but in the distance he noticed a buggy approaching, as it seemed to him, rather fast. As it got nearer, he could see that the vehicle rocked from side to side. Yes, it was a runaway, and a wild one at that. Dick turned a quick glance up the road. There were no teams in sight, but, a few rods ahead, a railroad crossed the street, and he could see the smoke of an approaching train coming round the curve. The driver had stopped the car without waiting for a signal. Dick had just time to fling his coat off and leap to the ground ; and even in the act of doing so he recognized one of his father's horses and saw a broken rein dragging under the animal's feet. He did not dare to look beyond, where the old man sat, erect and rigid, in the swaying buggy, his keen eyes fixed upon that curling smoke, mind and body braced for the shock.

As the maddened creature dashed by, Dick flung himself across his neck, seized the bit with both hands, and jerked the iron curb together with a force that almost broke the jaw. Arrested by the sharp agony, the horse reared wildly, Dick kept his clutch upon the bits, and as he felt himself lifted in the air, he shouted : " Get out— quick—get out ! "

The horse came crashing down with one leg over the shafts, and Dick, flung free of the struggling beast, felt a deadly pain in his arm, heard the shrill whistle of the engine as the train thundered over the crossing, and then he felt and heard no more. As his father lifted him in his

DICK.

arms, the bell-punch dangled heavily across the old man's knee, but the conductor's cap lay crushed beneath the feet of the men who had hurried to the spot to disentangle the frightened horse.

After all, a broken arm is no great matter, and Dick had much and various cause for thankfulness. But it was long before Dick's father could think with composure of that short but awful moment.

The next morning, as they sat together in the library, the disabled arm in a sling, the owner of the arm somewhat pale, but very happy, Dick learned of the business opening which had been preparing for him. His father did not tell him how, in his wrath, he had already taken steps toward cancelling the negotiations with his friend the manufacturer. Dick, however, suspected it, and his mother, who had borne the brunt of her husband's " state of mind " on that trying yesterday, sat by, in blissful mood, once more rendering thanks for a great deliverance.

Mr. Spencer was old-fashioned enough to give his son much good counsel on this occasion, to which Dick listened with unbounded faith and respect. His father wound up by saying: "When I went into business, my uncle, William Pratt, gave me one bit of advice which covers the whole ground. He said : ' It 's not so much matter what you do, Richard, so you do it devilish well.' "

Then, with a sudden burst of magnanimity, the old man added, "We 'll forget that wretched conductoring business as fast as possible; but I will say, Dick, that you did it 'devilish well.'"

"And nothing 'became him like the leaving it.'" Mrs. Spencer added, with glistening eyes, as she laid her hand gently on Dick's bandaged arm.

"Ah, Dick, you beggar," said his father rather huskily, and getting up from his chair with the instinct of flight, "that 's something we can't talk about."

"Oh, I say," Dick cried, growing very red in the face, "don't be so awful good to a fellow. I ought to have been thrashed."

And all having thus made a clean breast of the matter, these three warm-hearted people began to feel a little shamefaced, and with one accord endeavored to dispel the emotions which their Puritan blood made them shy of acknowledging.

Then Dick told his father and mother about Julie.

UNCLE BOBBY.

XIII

UNCLE BOBBY.

UNCLE BOBBY was a poet. That was why he had made a failure of life; that was why his hair had grown gray in an unequal contest with the realities of this prosaic world.

Uncle Bobby was a poet. That too was why his latter days were days of pleasantness and peace. Life, like a wise mother who has disciplined her child, took him gently by the hand and gave him of her best and sweetest. For the best and sweetest is not a matter of circumstance —it is not even success and love. It is being in tune. And Uncle Bobby was in tune like an instrument whose strings have yielded to a master hand. To-day he was sitting in his "yacht," as he had dubbed his tiny row-boat, his oars balanced idly, floating with the tide up the saltwater creek behind Pleasant Point. A stranger might not have guessed that he was a poet. From his gray felt hat slouched comfortably against the sun, down to the huge rubber waders encasing feet and legs, there was nothing æsthetic to be discovered. Corduroy trousers, to be sure, when judiciously cut, and especially if pausing just below the knee, may have a genial air. But the dingy corduroys worn by Uncle Bobby were not of a genial cut, nor did they disappear into the waders with any promise of stopping short of the solid, matter-of-fact instep of their owner. As to the alpaca sack-coat, it may be doubted whether any cut could lend an air of distinction to that highly inappropriate material, while even the picturesque possibilities of a gray flannel shirt were quite lost beneath an ancient black vest, from the pocket of which dangled an old-fashioned fob.

Furthermore, Uncle Bobby's face was of that florid cast which is manifestly unpoetic, and his blue eyes, not over large, were more inclined to lend themselves to fun than to inspiration. There was always a twinkle lurking somewhere in the background, ready to come to the surface, as promptly as the ripple stirs a quiet sheet of water at the faintest whisper of a summer breeze. Uncle Bobby's nose, a prominent feature, was also florid, and its rich tone was finely set off in contrast with the thick gray moustache which was its nearest neighbor. This moustache was military in its character, and of a darker, sterner hue than the benignant white hair, which was soft and fine as silk. On the whole, though not a poetical-looking personage, Uncle Bobby, in spite of his old clothes, might fairly have been called "a fine figure of a man." Tall and erect, though portly, too, he might easily have passed muster as an army officer, while as judge of the supreme court, he would have made a highly creditable appearance. But as a poet? No. Not by the last stretch of imagination could he have been dressed or drilled or dragged into the remotest semblance of a poet. As he sat there, idly drifting up the creek, and looking rather cumbersome in his little boat, which he maintained was "just a fit," he held between his teeth a small brierwood pipe. The pipe had gone out, but it was evidently at home in the situation.

There was another thing about Uncle Bobby. He had never in his life written a line of poetry, nor did he often read any. If he had done so, he would probably have admired the wrong things, things wherein sentiment predominated over imagination, things about old blind organ-grinders or broken-hearted maidens, or possibly the story of some faithful dog, starving to death on his master's grave. He had no taste, for instance, for descriptions of natural scenery with moral reflections thrown in. Especially poems descriptive of the sea failed to interest him. His friends would sometimes enclose in their letters cuttings from the " Poet's Corner," in which the English language was exhausted in the well-meaning effort to conjure up a vision of the sea to the reader's mind. Uncle Bobby politely admitted that the description was somewhat like the ocean, but then, the ocean was not one bit like the descrip-

tion ; and he would forget the futile verses in a
wordless reverie upon that great, changing, musical, living poem spread out before his chamber
windows, whispering to his tiny boat, drawing
his thoughts away, far beyond the thought of the
vast sea itself, out and beyond, where imagination
grew dim in horizons that no ship has ever neared.
And so it will be seen that Uncle Bobby, in spite
of his imperfect equipment, was a poet—was a
poet to-day even, as he sat with his pipe between
his lips, drifting with the tide up into the heart
of the marshes.

A small cat-boat went tacking across his stern.
Uncle Bobby left his oars to the care of the patent
row-locks, and their blades touched the water,
sending up a little shower of jewels on either side.

" Ah there ! " cried Uncle Bobby, taking his
pipe from his lips.

" Ah, there, Uncle Bobby ! "

" Bound for Great Isle ? "

" Ay, ay ! "

The cat-boat slipped slowly away on a new
tack, and Uncle Bobby, much refreshed by the en-
counter, proceeded to knock out the dead ashes
against the boat-side and stow the pipe away for
later service. Then he took to his oars and
rowed in a leisurely manner up the stream. He
looked about from time to time with the quick
eye of the sportsman, but the gun at his feet was
really there more for the sake of company than
for anything else. It was not the time of day for

sport. The tide, with its beautiful impartiality, sometimes sides with the birds—too often, Uncle Bobby thought, and he would hardly have admitted that the game might be of a different opinion. Uncle Bobby was a tender-hearted man, but "yellow-legs" and plover, black duck and "old-squaws," were so clearly invented for purposes of sport that he firmly believed that they too were quite in the spirit of it.

The tide had paused, as it does when at the highest, and Uncle Bobby paused too. Again he let his oars rest on the water, while he took off his hat and wiped his brow. His forehead within the line of the hat was white as snow. "Jest like his soul," old Marm Hawkins used to say. "Uncle Bobby's soul 's jest as white as a baby's, where 't ain't ben roughened up by this wicked world that was allers sot agin him. Ef Uncle Bobby 'd allers lived long of us, they never 'd ha' ben a mark on him, an' I don' know 's they 's any marks on him now. When he fust come down to stay at Jenkinses, he used to hev his ups an' downs, same 's the rest of us, an' he war n't allers sech good compny 's the Lord meant him for. But now! Lord a massy! He 's jest like an innicent child, with his kind heart and ludikerous sayins. They ain't nobody I 'd ruther smoke a pipe with, than Uncle Bobby!"

And many a pipe the two cronies smoked together by the side of Marm Hawkins's air-tight stove.

20

Uncle Bobby had not always borne that engaging title. In his days of feverish striving he had been known as Robert Pratt, the Visionary. From the time when, hardly more than a baby, he had delighted in his mother's singing of stirring old ballads, from the time when she, a visionary like himself, had talked to him of a wonderful future, he had had great ambitions. The poet that was in him then, as now, saw all the possibilities of happiness and success that life has in its gift, and the impulse onward and upward and outward was very strong. But the world is too prosaic for poets to deal with, and so Robert Pratt failed. It seemed a pity, for he had many talents; too many, perhaps. He played, by instinct it seemed, all the musical instruments he could lay hands on, his gift of mimicry was something wonderful, he was full of mechanical ingenuity, and even in matters of finance he had flashes of insight, which, joined to a practical shrewdness that was lacking, would have been the making of his fortune. But alas! he lost more money than ever he made; his inventions fell just short of the mark; his music never made itself heard in the world.

Yet why should one say alas? Would any degree of success, of wealth, of reputation, have put him in tune as he was to-day,—musing in his boat, looking abroad on the marshes? Would a successful man have found time to sit there rocking with the turning tide, bathing his soul in the sunshine and the beauty of the quiet hour? Would a rich man have felt the pride of owner- ship in all that exquisite color, in those reaches of marsh and of sea ; would a famous man have been left in peace, day after day, to live his own life and think his own thoughts, with no more importunate neighbor than old Marm Hawkins with her quavering voice and hobbling step? Uncle Bobby did not know he was a poet. He did not know that the deep content in which he habitually dwelt was something rare in this rest- less world. He did not know that the smell of the salt air was more delicious to him than to others, that the country side was fairer, the sea wider, the old lobster houses and fishing-smacks prettier in his eyes than in the eyes of his neigh- bors. He often looked wistfully down the vista of years to the distant past, and he fancied it fairer than the present. But then he had the past, too, as a part of the poem of life. Down that dim vista shone one sweet girlish face, one sweet girlish voice echoed low and clear. More than forty years ago that voice had been hushed, that face had been shut away from the sun, yet death could not complete his conquest over gentle Annie Wells so long as her old lover lived.

Uncle Bobby was a bachelor, but he did not feel in the least like one. What had he in common with those loveless beings who grow old and cranky in the pride of celibacy? He, for his part, had no patience with old bachelors.

There was a certain little poem which Uncle Bobby wore always in his pocket. When the paper became thin and yellow he had sewed with his own hands a silk covering for it, and that in its turn was worn and faded. The poem was one which Annie had cut out of a newspaper and given him a little while before she died. These are the words :

"Lean closer, darling, I must speak
    So very, very low.
Lean closer, till I touch your cheek
    And feel your tears that flow.

"Lean closer, dear, for I must try,
    Though it should break my heart,
To say the cruel word good-bye
    Ere you and I do part.

"Yet hush ! my darling, heard you not
    An echo faint and far,
From fairer futures half forgot,
    Beyond the evening star?

"Beyond the wondrous evening star,
    Where all is joy and peace,
'T is there good-byes are faint and far,
    Where welcomes never cease."

A poor little poem enough, but the one poem in the world for Uncle Bobby. Years ago he had set these words to music, and words and music had blended into something so very beautiful to his mind, that he had written them out and had them published. But when his cousin Arabella Spencer sang the song to him in her well-meaning but inadequate treble, he had experienced a sudden horror of what he had done, of the harsh treatment his modest little song would have to bear, and he had withdrawn the edition, and that was the end of his musical career. Only ten copies had been sold, and he hoped they might soon be lost.

The music sometimes haunted him, but to-day it was far from his thoughts. His mood was purely contemplative. Not a single long-drawn breath of the brimming creek escaped him, not a motion of the tall marsh grass, standing shoulder high in the pulsating tide. He watched, with quiet amusement, the elaborate twistings and windings of an eel among the sea-weed, the business-like preoccupation of a wicked old crab in the muddy ooze below, and when a soft-breasted sea-swallow alighted on the stern of the boat, an indescribable look of tenderness came into Uncle Bobby's blue eyes, and he sat motionless until the light-winged visitant had departed. The "yacht" had turned with the tide, and was drifting homeward, guided only by an occasional dip of the right oar or the left.

As she touched the beach Uncle Bobby planted his big waders in the water, and went splashing up the incline, hauling the boat up beyond high-water mark, where he dropped a miniature anchor in the sand. Then he made everything ship-shape in the tidy little craft, which was perhaps the best beloved of his sea-side cronies. He unscrewed the revolving seat, which he had ingeniously made out of the skeleton top of an old music-stool. "That's so that I can have the game handy if they fly the wrong way," he would explain; adding, confidentially, "Game are so flighty."

In the stern of the "yacht" was a snug little locker, where he stowed away his cartridges and his tobacco cuddy, and where a brandy flask and a box of crackers lay in wait against possible fogs. Here was also a small tin box which was usually well-stocked with checkerberry lozenges; his *bonbonnière* he called it, with a grand flourish when he offered it to lady passengers. The "yacht" was too small for the accommodation of more than one passenger, but when Uncle Bobby was socially inclined he would organize a little fleet, and with his own boat as flag-ship, would escort a picked party from the boarding-house up the creek; or, if the day was exceptionally calm, they would put boldly out to sea and make for Great Isle, a couple of miles to the northward. No one else could get up such a party at Pleasant Point, for no one else could wheedle the fishermen into cleaning up their boats and letting them out. It was a treat to see Uncle Bobby deal with the cantankerous owner of a jolly little "cat." He would saunter up to the water's edge, just as the man was trying to think of a new "cuss-word" for an ugly wind which twisted the ropes out of his hands as he was trying to make things fast.

"Good-morning, Mr. Kimball," Uncle Bobby would shout at the top of his voice ; "the *mosquitoes* seem to be plaguing you ! "

"Mr. Kimball," otherwise known as " Pickerel Pete," would look up with a wintry grin, and shout back, "At it again, Uncle Bobby ! " Upon which Uncle Bobby would wade out through the foaming shallows and lend a hand.

"Well-mannered little craft that," he would say, giving a neat twist to a rebellious rope. "I 've got a friend who would give his best hat to take her out some morning."

"Prettiest cat-boat on the shore," would be the next observation, as the two, having subjugated the rigging, tramped heavily in their wet boots across the sand. "I say, Mr. Kimball, you 're a good judge of the weather. Think this kind of thing 's going to last ? "

"Last ? Bless you, no ! It 's only a fair-weather breeze. We shall have a mill-pond outside by to-morrow morning. What caper have you got on hand for to-morrow ? "

"Oh, nothing but a little picnic, if we can get hold of the boats. Don't s'pose, now, you 'd spare yours, Mr. Kimball ? "

"Yes you do, Uncle Bobby. You s'pose I 'd be jest fool enough to let your fine, stuck-up city friends have her. You 're countin' on 't sure 's a gun."

"Well, I 'm much obliged to you, Mr. Kimball. I always thought you were the most accommodating man on the shore. We shall start about eight o'clock. And, I say, Captain," as the fisherman beat a retreat into his own cottage, "don't forget to send along the mosquito-netting. They 're pretty thick between this and Great Isle."

But if Uncle Bobby enjoyed an occasional junketing, he liked better still, for the most part, to "gang his ain gait." And he never felt better satisfied with the way his time had been passed, than when he had spent a morning up the creek with his gun for company. To-day he knew that Mrs. Jenkins had been preparing one of her clam-chowders, which, to Uncle Bobby's palate, amply represented soup and fish, solids and sweets. There was a time when Uncle Bobby aspired to champagne and French cookery to his dinner, —before he really knew his own tastes and needs. That was long ago, when he thought he must have Italian opera, though he should never hear again the deep baritone of the surf or the twitter of the sea-swallow; when he fancied he must own richly framed oil paintings, over which no changing lights nor brooding shadows ever swept. He had not heard so much as a concert now for several years, and all his pictures, save one, had been sold. That one was a chromo which he had picked up at auction for a dollar and a half, frame and all. The chromo had done for him a service which, as all are agreed, lies outside the province of art. It had taught him a lesson.

It came about in this wise, long before the Pleasant Point days. Uncle Bobby had been speculating rather wildly. He had an impression that riches were power. He did not know precisely how he should use such power if he had it, but he thought he should like to have a try at it. The child who chases a will-o'-the wisp till he is knee-deep in a swamp, does not know what he wants of it. It is bright and it dances away from him. Therefore he covets it. And Uncle Bobby, who was in very comfortable circumstances, who had not a chick nor a child to give his money to, nor any definite purpose for it whatever, had a notion that he wanted to be rich. So he risked everything in a "big venture," and when that failed, he sold his horses and sent his piano and his pictures to auction. He happened in on the day of the sale and was strongly tempted to bid high on his own possessions. Then his eye fell upon the chromo. It represented a man standing on the brink of a stream fishing. He had hooked a huge fellow whose weight was breaking the rod. In his agitation he had upset a basket, out of which poured a stream of little fishes, joyfully wriggling back into the water. His hat had blown off and was floating down stream, his coat was bursting out under the arms, and in his flushed face and staring eyes was all the excitement of the gambler who has staked everything on a losing game. Uncle Bobby gazed, fascinated, at the picture, and when it was put up for sale he was the only bidder, and he got it cheap.

This happened in New York, whither he had drifted in his quest after wealth and fame, and in that human wilderness he lived the life of a hermit for many years, years of dull routine, sometimes in the employ of a fickle government, sometimes in no employ at all. Occasionally, when he signed his name, he was reminded of all the prosperous, well-to-do Pratts, who had been content to lead reasonable lives in his native town of Dunbridge. After the death of his mother—that gifted and fascinating Emmeline Pratt whose memory was still green in the paths she had trod, —there was no tie strong enough remaining to draw him back to his own people. The most genial of men in prosperity, he felt a shrinking from old associations, now that he had made a failure of the game of life. He could still crack a joke with his landlady or the bootblack; he could still toss a coin from his scanty store to cheer a beggar; but, for his own part, he was a hermit in a wilderness, in that waste of brick walls and smoky air which is so much drearier than nature's wildernesses.

There came a time when Uncle Bobby fell ill, and had to keep his bed. As he lay there, passing in review the twenty cheerless years since he had had anything in particular to live for, he rather wondered that he did not wish to die. His chief diversion in the lonely days of convalescence was the contemplation of the old chromo which hung on his chamber wall. He thought he had learned its lesson pretty well. He had resisted the temptation to speculate with the small sum saved from the wreck of his fortunes, though it scarcely yielded him his board and lodging. In those days of slowly returning health, he took a grim pleasure in looking at the desperate fisherman on the bank. That wretched gambler was clearly losing his foothold on the very ground beneath him, and was slipping down into the stream. He, at least, Robert Pratt, had kept his head above water.

One morning his reflections took another turn. What good sport it used to be to go fishing! How many years it was since he had had any sport at all! And with a rush of memory the old days of his youth came back to him, when he used to go "down East" for a summer holiday. The more he thought about it the more his thoughts clung to the old memories, the more ardently he longed for the old delights.

Ten days from that time Uncle Bobby came, a travel-stained pilgrim, to Pleasant Point—travel-stained from the long and weary journey of life.

Human things had changed a good deal at Pleasant Point. The few straggling fishermen's huts had given place to a collection of tidy green and white cottages, a flourishing boarding-house had sprung up, where sportsmen with their wives and daughters were wont to congregate. The "Old Shanty" up the creek, where young Bob Pratt and his boon companions had many a time gone to camp out, had disappeared to the last shingle.

Robert Pratt, grown old in mind and body since those days, rowed up the creek and landed at the foot of the little bluff where the Old Shanty once stood. He wore his city clothes, and smoked a cigar. He looked out across the creek and the tongue of land built up with cottages, and there, over beyond, was his old friend, the ocean.

Yes, human things had changed ; but what of that ? Robert Pratt had had enough of human things. What he wanted now was something genuine and permanent. And there was the faithful coast-line, strong and unchanged, the ocean, gleaming blue beyond the pine-trees that fringed the beach. He knew their breath was as sweet as of old ; he could almost hear the murmuring sea-breeze among their storm-wracked branches. He watched the sea-gulls circling in the sun, the sails standing out white or gray against the horizon. Once more he felt the strong tonic of the salt air with its bountiful renewal. There was an exhilaration in it all which he had not known for years. He laid his hat down on the low-creeping junipers, and let the air sweep his brow. Suddenly the lapping of the tide on the rocks below struck his ear and touched his heart. The tired eyes filled, and for a moment the sunny day was veiled to his sight.

It is not often that such a thing happens to a man of sixty, a man too, not given to self-pity. When it does it may mean many things. To-day it meant that Robert Pratt in his city clothes would smoke no more cigars on the site of the Old Shanty. After that it was Uncle Bobby with his brierwood pipe who lingered among the junipers. He would take his New York *Herald* up there, and read of the doings of men in the world outside, and that echo of worldly turmoil only deepened the sense of security and peace. The fishermen sailing by, and the boys and girls out on a picnic, got the habit of looking up as they passed that particular bluff, hoping to catch a sight of Uncle Bobby's paper gleaming in the sun.

"Boat ahoy, Uncle Bobby!" the shrill voices would call, and Uncle Bobby would stand up, and wave his New York *Herald*, which fluttered as gayly in the breeze as though it were not black with the record of sins and follies of thwarted ambitions and cruel successes. And likely as not a jest would drop down among them, a jolly, good-humored jest that would not lose its relish all day long.

Uncle Bobby's jokes were considered wonders of wit. In fact there was nothing like Uncle Bobby's fun unless it was his kindness. He was hand in glove with every Pleasant Pointer, big and little, and welcome as the sun at every cottage door. "There comes Uncle Bobby!" the youngsters would cry, and leave their play to hear him talk. It was just like going nutting in the fall. You never could tell when a great bouncing joke might come popping plump onto your own head. The comparison was suggested to the more imaginative among the children by Uncle Bobby's avowal that the jokes were, half of them, chestnuts. "We like chestnuts," sturdy Billy Jenkins maintained, and all the boys and girls were of the same mind. But Uncle Bobby did himself injustice. He made more new jokes than old ones. Funny notions were constantly coming into his head. Since he had become an out-and-out Pleasant Pointer his humor was so gay, the sunshine had so saturated his being, that the gleams and glints were always going on in his brain.

Uncle Bobby was no "summer boarder" at Pleasant Point. He and the old chromo were fixtures there. He occasionally spent a winter month with his Dunbridge relatives, but though it seemed very pleasant and "folksy" among them, now that he had made his peace with life in general, yet he was always glad to get back to Pleasant Point with its whistling storms and tossing surf. He did not live at Ormsby's, the big boarding-house, but with Sol Jenkins, a prosperous householder who ran the express wagon out over the causeway to the railroad station twice a day. He brought in the mail and any stray passengers who were not otherwise provided for. Sol was an all-round genius of the variety rarely found out of Yankeeland, and Uncle Bobby delighted in him, as he had never delighted in brother or friend before. Sol's droll sayings and dry philosophy were better than all the books, and his ingenious doings as good as a play.

Mrs. Sol Jenkins was a famous cook, and just the kindest woman in the world, or so Uncle Bobby said. It was really surprising how many of the kindest and smartest people in the world Uncle Bobby discovered at Pleasant Point. The side of folks that was turned toward him always blossomed and bloomed as plants do toward the sun.

Now on the day when Uncle Bobby drifted up the creek and back again—the day when the sea-swallow twittered his little lay on the stern of the boat,—there was a new arrival at the boarding-house, a handsome, stately woman attended by a retinue of friends. And by the time Uncle Bobby had made fast the "yacht" on the beach behind the village, and was strolling homeward in the well-founded hope of a clam-chowder, the rumor had gone abroad, that the new arrival was no other than Kate Alton, the great contralto singer, whose fame had reached even Pleasant Point. There was a flutter of excitement through-

out the little community, for Miss Alton's good-
nature was almost as well known and almost as
phenomenal as her voice. Yet Uncle Bobby, who
had seen something of prima donnas in his day,
hardly thought it likely that she would sing,
and after supper he betook himself with his pipe
to Marm Hawkins's for a quiet smoke. Uncle
Bobby liked to sit out-of-doors in the pleasant
August evenings, but then, Marm Hawkins
liked his company in her stuffy little "settin
room," and without thinking much about the
matter, Uncle Bobby found it about as natural to
indulge his old neighbor's whims as his own.
So there he sat, enveloped in a cloud of tobacco
smoke, discussing the weather and the vagaries
of the deep-sea fish, when a messenger came to
summon him to Ormsby's—Miss Alton had con-
sented to sing.

"Has she sung anything yet?" asked Uncle
Bobby, as his feet crunched the powdered white
shells of the road.

"No! I guess not. She seemed to be un-
furlin' her main-sail when I come away. It
takes them big craft some time to git under
weigh."

But as they approached Ormsby's a superb
voice came sweeping out into the twilight. Uncle
Bobby stopped to listen, while his companion
trudged on ahead. The music rose and fell like
the very bosom of the deep, and a hot flush
burned on Uncle Bobby's cheek.

"Gad! but she can sing," he muttered to himself, as the song ended and he hurried forward. As he came up the piazza steps he saw that there was bright lamplight and a crowd of people in the parlor. Outside the air was sweet and cool, and the darkness was already creeping over the waters. Uncle Bobby sat himself down in a chair close to one of the open parlor windows. He could hear the murmur of conversation within, and a rustle of dresses, as the people discussed their small impressions of that great voice. Uncle Bobby sat, still smoking his pipe, looking out across the open ocean.

Presently a hush fell upon the company, and a clear voice said: "Now I am going to sing for you my favorite song."

A strangely familiar chord was struck, melting then away into a plaintive succession of notes. Uncle Bobby took his pipe from his mouth and started forward, with an intent look on his ruddy face. The quiet prelude ceased and there was an instant's pause. Then the voice of the great singer murmured rather than sang:

> "Lean closer, darling, I must speak
> So very, very low."

The simple words floated out on the music with a thrilling pathos that was almost too poignantly sweet to bear. Within the room the people held their breath to listen, while the white head outside sank forward, till the light from the

21

parlor window fell upon it like a halo. The music was singularly beautiful. In that hour Uncle Bobby felt it, though he almost forgot that it was his own. Then came the change in the harmony—that change which had made his heart beat high when first it dawned in his brain. The noble voice rose to its full volume, and rang forth on the words

" Beyond the wondrous evening star,"

melting again into a vibrating sweetness with the last line,

" Where welcomes never cease."

For an instant after the final chord died away no one spoke or moved. Then there was a burst of applause. When it ceased, Uncle Bobby heard the singer answering questions. He wished she would not put that voice of hers to such a prosaic use as talking. He drew back in his chair, that he might not be seen from within.

" I don't know anything about the composer but his name," Miss Alton was saying.

" But where did you get the piece ? " asked a summer boarder, who " sang a little herself."

" I found it among some old music of my mother's. I came across it when I was a young girl, and I fell in love with it. Indeed, I was singing that song when it first came over me that I had a voice."

" Won't you sing it again ? " some one begged.

Miss Alton laughed.

"I thought you would ask me to," she said. "I never yet sang it to an audience that I did not have a recall, and I always repeat the song, because I know that is what they want."

And then she sang it again, and it sounded even more beautiful than before. Uncle Bobby looked forth across the sea, to where a golden planet shone out, and a sudden calm fell upon him, as though he had known all along how beautiful his music was, and as though it really made no very great difference that others had found it out, since it was good music either way.

Again the applause was sounding in his ears, and now Uncle Bobby's mind had wandered from the music to the star, that was burning clearer every moment. Suddenly he heard his name.

"Yes," Miss Alton had been saying, "the publisher is dead, and I have never been able to find out anything about Robert Kingsbury Pratt. I am afraid he is dead too."

Here other voices took up the name. "Robert Kingsbury Pratt! Why, Uncle Bobby's middle name begins with a K!"—and cries of "Uncle Bobby! Uncle Bobby! Where's Uncle Bobby!" rose on every hand.

Then Uncle Bobby got up from his chair, and stole noiselessly across the piazza, and out, under the pine-trees to the white beach, where he paced up and down in the starlight. There was no moon, and there was little danger of his being discovered in the dim light. For hours he paced there, smoking his pipe out several times. The tide came creeping up to his feet and then it receded. He followed the water-line as it withdrew down the shore. His feet made scarcely a mark upon the firm sand. The shining star rose toward the zenith where it was lost among a host of others. And still Uncle Bobby paced the beach and smoked his pipe.

The next day, as Uncle Bobby, in his waders, with his oars over his shoulders, walked across the Point to the shore of the creek, where his boat was moored, he had many questions to answer about that song. He agreed that there was a curious coincidence in the names, but when pressed to give his middle name he gravely said it was Ketchum. Then he pushed his " yacht " off, got aboard her, and disappeared for an all-day trip.

Strange to say, Uncle Bobby's prevailing thought throughout the day, was of his late grandmother, the redoubtable Old Lady Pratt, and of her pride in the Kingsbury connection. " And I said it was Ketchum ! " he told himself remorsefully from time to time, feeling more like a culprit than he had done for many a long year. Yet his reflections ended each time in a self-congratulatory chuckle, after which he would draw a long, low whistle, and fall to examining the gun at his feet.

The people of Pleasant Point never found out

whether Uncle Bobby really knew anything about the song that had so enchanted them, and after a while they forgot it.

But Miss Alton seemed to have lost her heart to Pleasant Point, and she used often to come down for a week in the summer. She said it was "so restful." In the course of time she had many a checkerberry lozenge out of Uncle Bobby's *bonbonnière*, and sometimes, as they rowed home in the early twilight, a wonderful contralto voice might be heard winging its way across the quiet waters of the creek.

When the evening star shone out above Uncle Bobby's head, Miss Alton used to think to herself that the weather-beaten old hat looked exactly like a laurel crown.

www.ingramcontent.com/pod-product-compliance
Lightning Source LLC
Chambersburg PA
CBHW021110270326
41929CB00009B/813